Thought Transference: A Critical and Historical Review of the Evidence for Telepathy, with a Record of New Experiments 1902-1903

Northcote Whitridge Thomas

Thought Transference

A Critical and Historical Review of
the Evidence for Telepathy, with
a Record of New Experiments
1902–1903

By
NORTHCOTE W. THOMAS, M.A.
Author of "Crystal Gazing"

NEW YORK
Dodge Publishing Company
23 East 20th Street

COPYRIGHT, 1905, BY
DODGE PUBLISHING CO.

PREFACE

SINCE the foundation of the Society for Psychical Research more than twenty-three years ago, a great mass of more or less well-evidenced material has been published upon subjects such as thought-transference, crystal gazing, ghosts, mediumship, physical phenomena and other so-called " occult " manifestations. There have, however, been but few attempts to sum up the evidence and make it available for the ordinary citizen who cannot find time to read the whole of the thirty volumes published by the Society. Even in the Society's own publications there is, as a rule, no periodical summing up of the evidence for the various phenomena and hypotheses.

I propose, therefore, to discuss Psychical Research or Metapsychics, as Professor Richet terms it, in a series of works which will deal critically but sympathetically with the evidence. Where the historical and anthropological facts are of interest or importance, they will not be neglected, but my main purpose is to show what a reasonable

v

man without bias in either direction may regard as proved.

The ignorant criticism to which the Society was subjected in its earlier days has given place in many quarters to an equally uncritical acceptance of its results; but neither the credulity nor the scepticism of the public is based on knowledge. Denial and affirmation are both equally easy, when the authors of the sentiment know nothing of the question at issue. I hope to provide a series of text books which will render both scepticism and credulity less excusable.

I am much indebted to the various ladies and gentlemen whose trials are chronicled in the latter half of this volume, for assistance in experiments which are too often neither interesting nor successful. At the time of going to press I have lost sight of some of them, and their initials only are given in the absence of express permission to give the full names.

I am also indebted to the Council of the Society for Psychical Research for permission to quote from the *Proceedings* and *Journal*, and especially for the right of publishing the unprinted results of the experiments tried in 1901-2, the records of which are now in my possession.

NORTHCOTE W. THOMAS.

April, 1905.

CONTENTS

CONTENTS

CHAPTER I

Incredulity, scientific and otherwise—Action at a distance—The qualifications of a psychical researcher—Dr. W. B. Carpenter—What is science?—Objections to Psychical Research: its assumptions: its devotees: its sphere of enquiry

SOME things appear to us impossible because of the range of our knowledge. Few sane persons with a competent knowledge of physics will set out on a quest for perpetual motion. If by any chance such a person does do so, and believes that he has solved the problem, it is possible to demonstrate to him that his theoretical solution conflicts with established principles, and is therefore erroneous.[1] In other cases well-attested reports of phenomena are disbelieved, not because the statements contradict any positive knowledge, but by reason of the extent of our ignorance. Globular lightning was long regarded as impossible, not because it conflicted with any known facts, but

[1] A Cambridge wrangler was reported to have solved the problem some twenty years ago. The only defect in his solution was its omission to take account of the fact that gravity acts downwards.

because it was unlike any form of electric discharge that could be experimentally produced. As soon as it was shown that something analogous could be demonstrated in the laboratory, there was a change of view as to the value of the evidence previously accumulated.

In 1882 a Society, whose name is now a household word, was formed to conduct " an examination into the nature and extent of any influence which may be exerted by one mind upon another, apart from any generally recognized mode of perception," and for other objects. The Society for Psychical Research during the first ten years of its existence devoted its energies in the main to the question of thought transference or telepathy, spontaneous and experimental. Since that time the study of these questions has on the whole been overshadowed by investigations into trance mediumship —a line of research more attractive to the outside world, as well as to the spiritualistic section of the Society, but hardly calculated to be fruitful without at least a preliminary disproof of the existence of thought transference or a determination of its limits between living persons.

Since the experiments conducted in 1889 and 1890 by the late Prof. Sidgwick, Mrs. Sidgwick and others, no long series of trials has been published by the Society. Virtually no fresh evidence has therefore been accumulated, and in view of the experience of the possibilities of error gained since the childhood of the Society this failure to accumulate new evidence cannot but throw some doubt on results which at the time seemed almost conclusive. This doubt must in fact gain strength from the conclusive character of the evidence published in *Proc. S.P.R.* vi, 128; viii. 560, *sq.* If the Society has, in the twelve years which have elapsed, failed to obtain, in a series of any length, results that were above probability, or so much above probability as to exclude chance variations as a probable explanation, we can either conclude that the perceptual faculty is rarely possessed in the degree to which the Brighton percipients of 1889 and 1890, chosen, it appears, at random, possessed it, or we can perhaps with more reason conclude that there was some serious undetected flaw in the method of experimentation.

The purpose of the following pages is, in the first place, to give a brief sketch of the evidence so far available for experimental thought transference, and, in the second place, to indicate the lines on which those who have no special claim to acquaintance with the sources of error in psychological investigation, and who do not regard themselves as more favoured than their fellows in the direction of divining the thoughts of other people, may profitably (to science, if not to themselves) experiment, and to show in what respect such experiments, attended with but slight success, though they may be, from the point of view of those who regard thought transference as a fact to be proved by experimentation with exceptional individuals, may do more to establish the theory on a sound basis than all the more sensational work of previous investigators.

It has been pointed out above that there are two kinds of incredulity—one, which may be termed scientific, refuses to accept any evidence, however good in quality and quantity, which would, if accepted, involve the assumption that two contradictory statements can both be true. The other, which is pure prejudice and merely an example of scientific superstition, refuses to accept any evidence, however good in quality or quantity, as to facts or alleged facts, for no other reason than that they cannot be brought into line with, and shown to be analogous to, one or more accepted facts. In so saying, I do not, of course, include the sane scepticism which refuses to accept statements not backed up by sufficient evidence,[1] but only that attitude of mind which is so satisfied with its supposed

[1] The question of what is sufficient evidence is a difficult matter and need not be discussed here.

knowledge of the universe, as to be able to inform humanity that no evidence can be sufficient, that experiments in such matters are mere folly, and that no results can be anticipated from them (*vide Nature, vol.* 24, p. 172.) The irrational character of this attitude is apparent, when we reflect that were it logically adhered to, no evidence would suffice to convince us of the existence of any isolated fact in nature, however many observations were available. We might for example deny the existence of gravitation because it is the only force which appears to be independent, in its manifestation, of either time or space.

The scientific world (or certain members of it), has declared telepathy to be an impossibility; it has done this on the ground that action at a distance is impossible, and that therefore no hypothesis which involves it is worth consideration. With regard to these assertions, it may be noted that it is very far from proved that action at a distance is impossible. At most, what has been proved is that no action hitherto observed is action at a distance, and even this statement might require to be qualified in the case of gravitation, if not of other forces. However that may be, any one who maintains that action at a distance cannot be a fact because it has not yet been discovered, is no more advanced than the labourer, who, on seeing a steam-engine at work for the first time, concluded that there was a horse inside it because that was the only kind of non-human force that he knew. The savage and the scientist are not so far from one another as some people imagine.

It is, however, very far from proved that telepathy any more than gravitation involves action at a distance. It is, indeed, difficult to conceive how the vibration of a physical medium can transmit thought; but this is no more an objection to the view that it does do so, than is the impossibility of bridging the gulf from molecular motion to consciousness a refutation of the hypothesis that the brain is the organ of mind. We may reasonably go on to ask by what kind of reasoning it has been proved that consciousness is localized in the brain. A physicist tells us that a charge of electricity appears to be localized on the surface of a conductor, but is really distributed in space round it. We have absolutely no grounds for supposing that the same may not be true of consciousness. All arguments to the contrary assume that absence of sensation (I mean thereby, absence of one of the ordinarily recognized five sorts of sensation conveyed by definite nerves and under normal circumstances, definitely localized) is equivalent to absence of consciousness and that consciousness, so far as it is feeling, is the sum of the feelings conveyed by the nervous system.[1] This, however, is the very point at issue and cannot be assumed unless experiments devised to that end (which may be, as a matter of fact, impossible to conceive, or carry out) have proved that no such " distribution " of consciousness occurs.

We may again ask in what sense it can be said that consciousness is localized at all. We are, of course, made aware by our senses only of vibrations that impinge on the nerve ends, or in other words, impulses that directly affect the body. But that is no proof that localization can be intelligibly attributed to consciousness. If we are only conscious of heat or cold when the surface of the body is at a different temperature from its surroundings, that is no proof that our consciousness is at a temperature of 98.5°. To put the matter in another form, consciousness is certainly, so far as introspection tells us anything, non-spatial. We cannot therefore object to inquire into the possibility of one consciousness influencing another, through other than the recognized modes of sensation, on the ground that such influence necessarily involves action at a distance; spatial nearness and distance are mean-

[1] On this question the experiments in clairvoyance are of interest, by which I mean experiments such as those tried by Professor Richet (*Proc. S.P.R.*), to determine how far it is possible to guess cards drawn at random and unseen by any one.

ingless as applied to our own consciousness and do not necessarily apply to the relation of our own to other consciousnesses. The argument that telepathy involves action at a distance in this case falls to the ground.

Objections of this class fail, moreover, for the simple reason that no generalization from the facts of experience can exclude the possibility of other facts not inconsistent with the previously ascertained facts. That knowledge ordinarily and habitually comes to us one way no more excludes the possibility of its coming in an entirely different way, than the practically instantaneous discharge of electricity under ordinary circumstances excludes the possibility of globular lightning and other slow discharges. Congruent observations by competent observers must be accepted as *prima facie* evidence until definite sources of error are demonstrated.

This brings us to a second point. It is frequently argued that the proper persons to take up thought transference are physiologists, and that those who have no knowledge of the phenomena of brain or of mind are incompetent. It may be pointed out that no physiologist who ever lived could explain by means of physiology how we think at all. If the idea " cat " is associated with a certain molecular arrangement in the brain, all the professors in the world cannot tell us why it should be so associated, nor even tell us with what arrangement of the molecules of the brain the idea " cat " is associated. As thought transference deals with ideas, the physiologist is clearly no use, so far as explanations are concerned, though so far as physiologists are more likely to exclude errors and to experiment in the most scientific way possible, their work on the question of telepathy is desirable. But to argue that because a man has investigated the mechanism of the nerves or the minute structure of the brain, he is better qualified to discover the causes of certain states of mind, is an obvious absurdity. It does not follow that a physicist who understands the mathematics of the question will be a better shot than a gamekeeper or a poacher. Nor does it follow that a man whose experience has been with microscopes will be successful in dealing with the medium. The sole point on which his knowledge, as distinguished from his skill as an experimenter, will be useful is on the question of how far hyperæsthesia in the normal or the hypnotised subject can explain the phenomena and, perhaps, what precaution should be taken to exclude the possibility of it. Otherwise a physiologist is not necessarily of so much use as a phonographer. For under proper conditions of experimentation the sole question is, " Did the mental phenomena of the agent show a relation, not to be explained as the result of chance,

to the mental phenomena of the percipient?"
Given an accurate record of the psychical states·of
each, and it does not matter a halfpenny, so far
as the proof, as distinguished from the explanation
of telepathy goes, what their brain states are. For
the benefit of those, however, who put their faith
in the physiologist, it may be pointed out that, as
a matter of fact, more than one person to whom more
than common knowledge in such matters is attributed has investigated the question of thought transference and that their researches have not been un-
attended with success. As an example I may cite
Professor Richet, details of whose experiments in
hypnotism at a distance are to be found in *Proc.
S.P.R.,* v. 32, *sq.; Revue Phil.* xxv. 435.

A curious commentary on the alleged super-
excellence of physiologists as investigators in these
matters is supplied by a letter of the arch enemy of
spiritualism, telepathy, *et hoc genus omne,* the late
Dr. W. B. Carpenter, in *Nature,* June 30, 1881,
p. 188. He had given a testimonial of a sort to the
" thought reader," W. I. Bishop, and here narrates
an experiment, showing that " we may be guided in
our choice among things ' indifferent ' by *influences
of which we are ourselves unconscious.*" The experiment was this: the subject drew a card from a pack,
identified it, and returned it; the pack was shuffled
and sixteen cards dealt by the agent, face down-

wards in four rows; the subject then selected a row. According to Dr. Carpenter the selected row was to be taken away. It could not therefore, if the experiment was to be successful, contain the selected card; but this is a point on which some doubt is permissible. Three rows were selected in this manner and three cards of the remaining row, and the last card, on being turned up, was identical with the card originally selected. This experiment was performed with success before Dr. Carpenter three successive times, he himself being the subject on the last occasion. The selection of rows or cards was, in each case, made by the subject with his right hand, which Mr. Bishop held in his left, and Dr. Carpenter held that the influence was unconsciously conveyed by this means.

The explanation suggested by Dr. Carpenter is not very convincing, and an ardent believer in telepathy might be disposed to regard telepathic influence as a more likely hypothesis. We need not, however, go so far afield. The theory of Dr. Carpenter implies that Mr. Bishop knew which card had been selected; this of itself involves, if the trial is always successful, both trickery and some amount of conjuring; for in Dr. Carpenter's report we are not given to understand that any means were openly taken to secure that the selected card should be among those dealt; and even if such means were taken there would be nothing to show which was the card in question. But given this amount of deception, it is not apparent why we should hold that the remainder of the trick was performed in the way suggested by Mr. Bishop and accepted by Dr. Carpenter. In the first place, we do not learn that any precautions were taken to secure that the experiment was tried with an ordinary pack; the simplest way would obviously be to try it with one made up of fifty-two cards all alike, the company being allowed to inspect a second pack of the ordinary kind. If this was not the case, it remains to be proved that his agent did not sometimes change his formula and declare that the row or card selected was the row or card to be retained. Here again, success must obviously be certain. But even if this were not so, there is always that possibility of explaining away ill success, which is the chief resource of civilized mediums as of savage sorcerers; the agent could always declare, when the row containing the card selected had been removed, as it must frequently be, even if Mr. Bishop selected for his card a location likely to influence in his favour the choice of the subject, that the card was in the remainder of the pack, had never been on the table. We have therefore, at least three other possible explanations, none of which involve more than trickery of one sort or another, or a long study of the principles on which the ordinary man makes three successive choices; against this latter hypothesis tell Dr. Carpenter's three successes, if they are to be regarded as anything but an exceptional series. It is possible that Dr. Carpenter's theory is the correct one; but, if this is the case, he is clearly deficient in one, or perhaps two, of the most essential qualities of a psychical researcher. Either he took no precautions against the two former of his suggested methods; or, if he did, he did not record the precautions, which may or may not have been adequate. In any case the experiments, as recorded, are valueless.

A reviewer in the *Lancet*,[1] with that air of superiority which always endears a man to his fellow searchers, is willing to admit that psychical researchers have devoted their " abilities, such as they are," to the questions they have made their own. Such an expression might seem, in the mouth of any ordinary human being, slightly ludicrous, when it is used of a society which has included among its active workers Henry Sidgwick, Oliver Lodge, F. W. H. Myers. Doubtless, if the anonymous reviewer's name were at our disposal, we should discover that his attitude is amply justified. However that may be, the analysis of Dr. Carpenter's letter given above shows that even a physiologist, who has given special

[1] May 2, 1904.

and markedly hostile attention to the problems of spiritualism and thought transference and to occult questions generally, may be ludicrously at sea when he comes to deal with an investigation that would present no special features of difficulty even to the average psychical researcher, much less to the expert.

The fact is, the problems of psychical research are such, that very special training is necessary to enable even a clever man to deal with them successfully. This special training, added to general culture and an expert's acquaintance with some branch of science, provides us with the ideal psychical researcher; but, if for a special investigation there were available an acute experienced man of the world with no scientific training or an acute scientist with no special acquaintance with the problems with which he would have to deal, there can be no question but that the choice should not fall on the man of science. So much for the argument against Psychical Research which is based on the supposed inadequate education of its chief exponents.

Again, we have the objection that telepathic experiments are not such as can be repeated at will in the laboratory and that its methods and assumptions are unscientific. The chemist puts his faith in the results of his labours, because, given the same conditions, the same result will be produced, and he, as other men of science, claims that nothing is really scientific which does not admit of similar exact experimentation. This is, however, to shut one's eyes to the nature of science and to the distinctive characters of its branches. If we leave out of account mathematics, which, with logic, holds a peculiar position, owing to the fact that its subject matter is a pure abstraction, the sciences fall into three main groups: 1. the experimental sciences such as physics, where, in theory at any rate, all the conditions regarded as capable of influencing the result can be varied at will; 2. the observational sciences, such as astronomy, where none of the conditions can be varied at will; and 3. the mixed sciences, such as biology, where certain of the factors are amenable to variation at will, but the majority are at present beyond our control. The psychologist has to deal with a mixed science; but the mere fact that a given experiment cannot be reproduced at will is no more a proof that psychology is not a science than is the fact that the objects of the experiment may die and nip it in the bud, a proof that biology is not a science. The biologist can only select his subjects and vary the external conditions; his main business is the observation of processes over which he has no control and of the nature of which, in some cases, such as reproduction, he can form little or no idea. The bacteriologist can inject his serums and anti-toxins into selected subjects, but it is very problematical if he will always produce the desired result. And, above all, the doctor can dose his patients with medicines by the gallon and pills by the cartload and the outcome of it all is that the patient is worse and not better. Yet biology, bacteriology and medicine are regarded as sciences, pure and applied, and the experts on these subjects would feel themselves insulted if any one told them they were unscientific.

The fact is, that what distinguishes science from other branches of knowledge is neither the method nor the subject matter, but the aim with which the studies are pursued. Science is organized knowledge, and an inquiry is scientific if its object is to investigate in such a way as to arrive at general results, or results that, in combination with others, lead to general conclusions. Science must of necessity study the individual, but it does so in order to draw conclusions as to the species. The discovery of general laws is the aim of psychical research, no less than of other investigations into the other phenomena of mind and matter. Consequently it cannot, on this head, be urged that psychical research is unscientific. Using terms loosely, we are accustomed to speak of an inquiry, a method, or, more often, of an individual inquirer, as scientific or unscientific. By that is meant not that the phenomena which form the subject matter of the inquiry are outside the range of science; that is, properly speaking, impossible, if the definition of science just given is correct. Scientific in this sense refers to the assumptions with which the inquirer starts, to the exactness of his methods of experimentation, and of his manner of recording the conditions and results, to the ability or inclination of the student to consider all the data requisite to a just judgment, and to his capacity for deducing the conclusions from those data in a logical manner. Here, too, we have no ground for denying to psychical research the name of science. Its postulates differ in no essential particular from those of other sciences. If we are justified in assuming that the chemist, for example, can properly distinguish between the changes in his laboratory, which he regards as casually connected with other changes in the same locality, and all the other manifold changes in the rest of the universe; or that he can, in other words, class certain antecedents as causes, discard others as irrelevant, and again select certain consequents as the effects of these causes, and discard others as due to other, independent, causes, it does not appear that we can condemn psychical research for postulating the same possibility of isolating causes and effects.

c

The charge against psychical research is, however, not so much that its positive assumptions are mischievous. Its critics object that it does not assume enough. It does not assume that the postulates of physical science such as, that action at a distance is impossible—itself an unproved and unprovable hypothesis—necessarily apply to, or rather have any meaning in, the domain of psychical science. So far as this implies a readiness to consider " occult " theories in preference to explanations based on the principles to which physical science gives her adherence, it is to be censured, as is any other bias in the man of science, whose business is to go where his facts lead him. But it is clear that a bias in this direction is not a necessary part of the equipment of a psychical researcher. On the other hand, if the contention be admitted that physical science, which cannot now and perhaps never will be able to give an intelligible account of the relation between mind and matter, is entitled to lay down the law as to what is possible and what is not possible in the psychical domain, we are asked to adopt an utterly unproved hypothesis, or, in other words, to set out on our investigations with a bias against a certain class of explanation. It is not the absence of bias which is demanded of us; this simple statement is enough to justify the attitude of psychical research. In the last resort the charge against psychical research frequently resolves itself into one against the spirit of its devotees. Both its aim and its procedure may be scientific, but the average person who takes an interest in psychical research is not a psychologist and does not approach it from the psychologist's point of view. If this is a valid objection, we may with equal justice dismiss astronomy from the ranks of science, because the majority of people who look at the stars are not astronomers, or biology, because the cattle-breeder is interested in the question from a severely practical point of view, or medicine, because the interest of the layman in it is stimulated, not by a proper scientific spirit, but rather by a distressingly mundane desire to be rid of his pains. A retrospective census would be even more effective in defeating the claims of any branch of knowledge, judged on these principles, to the name of science. But no one is asked to listen to an incompetent person who chooses to dabble in psychical research, any more than any one is bound to give a hearing to an earth flattener, or a defender of Christian Science, or any other amiable lunatic, because they deal with the same phenomena as their more rational fellow-men who go by the names of professor, F.R. S., or doctor. If the aims and methods of an individual inquirer are scientific, no amount of unscientific fellow-workers can ever make them anything else.

In conclusion, we may take note of one other objection that has been brought against psychical research—that it unwarrantably separates from the domain of psychology facts properly falling within its sphere and takes an interest in a number of phenomena which are not psychical but physical in their nature and dependent on trickery for their production. As regards the first point, the *raison d'être* of all science is ultimately its utility to the human race. So far as knowledge is not useful, it comes under the head of mental gymnastics; for this kind of employment it is clearly immaterial what its subject matter is, so long as it provides sufficient scope for ingenuity. Psychology has, up to the present, shown no disposition to make its own the problems of psychical research; yet probably no one will be found to deny their importance; if it is unworthy of science to go into these questions, the most important of which is the evidence for what is generally termed immortality, or more properly for the persistence of personality after death, we can only feel surprise that astronomers have been permitted to prepare without rebuke the *Nautical Almanac,* and that men of science should be found so misguided as to believe that the task of relieving human suffering is not unworthy of a doctor.

So long as psychology considers it not only more important but its exclusive business, so far as experiment is concerned, to determine how many meaningless combinations of letters can be remembered and reproduced after a single perusal, or what is the smallest increment perceptible to the various senses, and similar soul-absorbing questions, so long, at least, will psychical research justify her existence, if no longer. But, be it noted, the kind of training which makes a man a competent psycho-physicist will not necessarily make him a good psychical researcher, though of course it will be helpful. Psychical researchers have deliberately mapped out for themselves a region into which no self-respecting man of science thought of penetrating in earlier days, or if one was so ill advised as to do so, he quickly learnt, like Sir William Crookes, how little right—in his fellow-scientists' eyes—he had to the name of scientific inquirer. The region may be ill-mapped and pathless, but that it is so lies at the door of that science which will not investigate for itself and would forbid others to undertake on its behalf the duty of determining how far the almost universal belief in the existence of something more than a purely physical man can be justified by scientific evidence.

That psychical researchers have to deal with tricksters is, in many cases, certain and, that being so, it follows that there is nothing psychological in the facts which are, in such cases, the subject of inquiry. But, in the first place, the facts are investigated in order to determine whether or not trickery is at the bottom of them. Psychical research can no more refuse to investigate a *primâ facie* case, because some sage may, after the event, declare that the facts were physiological and not psychological, than geology can refuse to examine a fossil that turns out to have been produced by human agency in the twentieth century, or than geography can refuse a hearing to a de Rougemont because he subsequently turns out to be an impostor. Even were it otherwise, though it is difficult to see how any science can be denied the rights of determining what facts properly fall within the sphere, psychical research has an important work to do in delivering mankind from superstition. A detailed analysis of a fortune-teller's predictions would, if it could be brought to the notice of her possible victims, be far more effective in securing them against her wiles, than all the police prosecutions in the world. A description of the methods by which a fashionable medium contrives to delude her sitters into a belief in her super-normal powers, whether she really has any such power or not, would perhaps, as a fairly extensive experience assures me, fail to carry conviction to their habitual clients, though it might debar others from falling into their clutches. A demonstration of the rules by which, only too often, trance and materializing mediums play upon the feelings of those who have lost friends near and dear to them, in order to make a profit out of the sorrow of the survivor and from their longing for a sign of continued existence of those who, it may be, are only gone before, would do more to uproot one of the most iniquitous traffics on the face of the earth, than all the scientific sermonizing imaginable about the folly of spiritualism and psychical research.

We recognize that dangerous drugs should not be used except under the advice of experts, and that the investigation of their qualities and physiological effects is a task for experts only. It is a true saying, though there may be exceptions to it, that a man who is his own lawyer has a fool for his client. If the world at large recognized the truth of this as applied to psychical research, and were content to leave the work of investigation to experts, and to submit themselves, when they are the subjects of investigation, to the conditions laid down by the expert, mankind would be taken in far less frequently and the truth in these matters would be reached far sooner.

No one would expect to get the better of an average conjurer, unless he were himself an expert in prestidigitation, and even then many tricks would refuse to yield up their secrets. Experience shows that even acute observers completely fail to give an accurate account of a seance with a conjurer. Their failure to do so renders an explanation of the trick by means of their report impossible or very nearly so. In psychological matters, likewise, everything depends upon accuracy, and accuracy is attainable only by training. It would be as reasonable to expect a botanist to conduct physical experiments with success as to look for light from the amateur in psychical research. The botanist recognizes that he is not familiar with physics but, just as the fact that economics is largely concerned with buying and selling deludes the average man into the belief that his opinion on fiscal matters is worth having, so the fact that every one is familiar with his own mental operations leads him to believe that his judgment on questions of psychology or psychical research is reliable. If the possession of a mind makes a man a psychologist, the possession of a body should make him an anatomist and physiologist. But here the man in the street draws the line.

CHAPTER II

Telepathy a designation, not a theory —Possible errors

TELEPATHY (and telæsthesia,[1] or, as they might be termed, telepsychy) is frequently spoken of as a hypothesis. Except in one sense, where it is opposed to a spiritistic interpretation of certain facts, which do not concern us here, this is an error; it is not a theory, but a designation. It does not profess to explain how certain phenomena are caused, but only states that they occur and that they do not appear to be due to certain well-recognized causes, with the working of which the man of science and the man in the street are comparatively familiar. It is therefore entirely beside the mark to demand, as Professor Jastrow[2] does, a telepathic theory which does not involve conceptions alien to physical science in the place of the hypothesis, which he conceives to have been put forward by those who have endeavoured to prove

[1] Telepathy is used in the active as well as the passive sense. It might be well to disregard its etymology and restrict it to the active sense.

[2] *Fact and Fable in Psychology*, p. 101.

experimentally the existence of thought transference, that postulates forces and a method of working
of which physics can form no conception. The
Society for Psychical Research was formed to
investigate, among other questions, the possibility
of, or rather the evidence for, an influence of mind
on mind exerted through other than the ordinary
channels of the senses. The mode or modes by
which such influence is exerted are provisionally
termed telepathy, and the agile mind of the professional scientist seems to have scented in the
word the deadly heresy of action at a distance.
As a matter of fact, the term no more implies
it than do the harmless, necessary telescope, telephone and telegraph. That the term does not
imply action at a distance does not of course mean
that it excludes it, but the evidence, if any, for
telergy must necessarily be subsequent to that for
telepathy. If science, for example, were ultimately
compelled to accept a theory of action at a distance
as an explanation of, let us say, gravitation, the
fact of gravitation would, it is clear, have been
established long before its explanation. In fact, to
any but a professional psychologist it might seem
obvious that, under ordinary mundane conditions, it is difficult to conceive of any other time
relation between a fact and its explanation.
It is clearly a somewhat illogical proceeding to

provide the explanation and then proceed to inquire if the fact to be explained exists. Psychical research endeavours to establish the fact of telepathy and might well be prepared to leave the explanation of it to future generations. This attitude, of course, by no means excludes the possibility that, side by side with the proof of telepathy may be put forward theories or suggestions as to the mode of action. These suggestions may be rankly heretical in scientific eyes, or again they may attempt to explain the supposed facts in terms of matter and motion. In either case, even if it be a scientific crime to attempt the explanation of a new fact, the preliminary investigation seems harmless enough. The heresy, if any, lies in the suggested explanation and not in the proof of the fact, which is all that psychical research, as officially defined, attempts to accomplish.

In a work which deals with the question solely from the experimental side, it is unnecessary to discuss the thousand and one sources of error to which we are exposed in collecting and dealing with spontaneous cases. There are, it is true, certain fairly obvious precautions necessary to ensure that no elements drawn from the ordinary sense perceptions formed the link between the mental states of the agent and the percipient, but these need not detain us long.

Only one serious source of error is likely to be present in reasonably cautious experiments— hyperæsthesia. We know little as to the ordinary limits of our sensory powers, and still less of their limits in the hypnotic and other abnormal states; indications imperceptible even to the trained observer, must always be reckoned with when agent and subject are in the same room, as an experience of M. Bergson will prove. He showed (*Rev. Phil.,* 1886, p. 527, that a hypnotised boy was able to recognize and read arabic figures reflected in his eye, when their total heights could not have been more than $\frac{1}{250}$ of an inch. More than one case has been recorded in which, by practice, a person has been able to recognize, apparently by touch, and name a card drawn at random from a pack. In this connexion it is important to notice that the subject is frequently, if not invariably, unable to say whence he derives his knowledge, and that the group of experimenters may, therefore, be *bona fide* quite in the dark as to the disturbing element in thought transference experiments and hit upon it, if at all, by chance.

The possibility of hyperæsthesia and subconscious interpretations of subconsciously perceived indications vitiates, or may vitiate, most, if not all, experiments where the subject and agent are within sight of each other, whether directly or indirectly, by the means of reflecting surfaces. In certain cases the indications may be auditory in their nature, though up to the present the so-called " unconscious whispering "[1] has never been proved to exist or to be a probable explanation of the results. In the place of a general discussion of the question, it will be more convenient to indicate in connexion with each experiment, or group of experiments dealt with at length, the possible sources of error under this head.

Leaving out of account fraud, which should be detected by any reasonably competent investigator, we have only one other source of error that need be here mentioned. This is what may be termed mental convergence. Ask a hundred persons to draw three diagrams, and the probability is that a majority will draw a circle, a square and a triangle. This source of error, and a cognate one, arising from the natural sequence of ideas in our minds, leading us to select numbers or draw diagrams in a certain order, which may be briefly termed a number-habit, or a diagram-habit, as the case may be, may, of course, according to circumstances, operate in such a way as to decrease the number of coincidences in the mental phenomena of the subject and agent, if their " habits " are different, or it may tend to act in the opposite direction.

[1] Cf. Lehmann and Hansen: *Ueber unwillkürliches Flüstern.*

These errors can, however, be easily provided against by ensuring that chance and not deliberate volition selects for us the diagram, card, number, or what not that is to be transferred. There may be, it is true, residual errors, if abnormalities in the cards or numbers lead to our unconsciously selecting precisely those which are favoured by the number or diagram-habit of the percipient. But this chance of error is fairly remote, and even the apparatus of a psycho-physical laboratory might not pass through the ordeal of an equally searching examination into possible defects, and whereas errors arising from convergence and divergence would be equally probable in a thought transference series where we have not to determine absolute values, the errors in the other case might be all in one direction.

A source of error sufficiently common in the early days of investigation into these matters— a possibility fully recognized by the S.P.R. from the first—was muscle-reading. It may be laid down without danger of serious error that any success in divining the agent's thoughts, where subject and agent are in contact, much more when they are hand in hand, is largely due to muscle-reading, and that the slight unconscious motions thus sensed and interpreted are alone sufficient to account for the bulk of the successes. There may be another element—the telepathic—but until telepathy is proved to be a fact, this cannot be assumed, and in any case the telepathic element must always remain a factor of uncertain value. Some of the successes may appear too striking to be due to muscle-reading alone, but we must consider that a considerable number of people have the power of automatic writing and drawing, that although they are as unconscious of what they are doing as if their hands belonged to a third person, they are no more unconscious than a third person, and may become dimly or clearly aware of the purport of the writing by directing their attention to the movements of their hands. If now an individual may, by writing, externalize the ideas in his brain, ideas perhaps only present subconsciously, and become aware of them before he reads the writing, it may be possible for another person, who has himself no share in the production of the writing, to do the same. But clearly the writing is, in both cases, an entirely subsidiary element in the case. The pencil might be pointless or non-existent and the externalization of the thoughts and interpretation of the signs be no less complete than before, though the collateral evidence in the shape of the writing would no longer be present to back up the interpretation of the muscular movements. Possibly an element of this description may have facilitated the more striking successes of the willing game.

However this may be, it is certain that no experiment where contact has been permitted is worth mentioning as evidence of telepathy. I therefore, include none such in the evidence which I consider in the present work.

CHAPTER III

*The subliminal—Ordinary sense perception—Hyp-
notic hallucinations—Trance—Clairvoyance*

THE details of the experiments and their import
will probably be more easily apprehended, if the
discussion of them is preceded by some account of
the meaning of the technical terms of psychical
research, the use of which cannot be avoided in the
following pages.

Although it does not figure largely in the present
work, we may begin with the subliminal—a term
familiar to all readers of the posthumous work of
F. W. H. Myers, *Human Personality*. His views
on the subject will, I hope, be expounded in another
volume of this series by a writer whose works on
psychical research have already done much to
popularize its ideas. Here it is not necessary to
say more than will serve as a groundwork for what
follows.

We become aware of the external world by means
of sense perceptions. These are due to the stimulation of the retina by light waves, of the ear by air
waves, of the various nerve endings in the ordinary

skin by heat, cold, or pressure, and so on. As we shall be mainly occupied with visual impressions in the following pages, to the exclusion of sensations of hearing, touch, taste and smell, we may narrow the field to be surveyed by confining ourselves to this kind of perception. When rays of light fall upon the retina, it by no means follows that we become aware that they are so falling, and this may be due to two causes. The rays of light may be in themselves too feeble to be appreciated, however much we may bend our mind to the task; or, on the other hand, our attention may be otherwise occupied, and the stimulation of the optic nerve, though sufficient to cause a change in our consciousness, does not in fact do so, because we are engaged in watching something else, or because impressions of another order, such as those of hearing or taste, crowd out the impressions of sight, at any rate to a considerable extent. To use a common phrase, we are, in respect of the impressions which fall unheeded, " absent-minded." There is a third reason why we may fail to take up into our everyday, waking consciousness, which we call our mind, the impressions which are transmitted by the nerves to the brain, they may be of too short duration to be understood; every one knows how difficult it is to read the name of a station when our train rushes through at full speed. In the case of air waves, we may be unable to distinguish the particular ones on which we concentrate our attention, because they are drowned by the multitude of other air waves falling on the drum of the ear. All these causes may be operative in our waking moments and in full possession of our ordinary waking consciousness.

We may also fail to perceive the nerve impulses, or perceive them only in a distorted and unrecognizable form because we are not awake. Messages from the external world do indeed reach us, and we are often living in a world which, while it lasts, often appears to us fully as real as the external world of our waking moments, but the world of our sleeping moments is the work of our minds, and the messages from the outside world are only incidental and do not necessarily play any part in calling into being our dream scenery and incident.

Again, we may be neither asleep nor, in the strict sense of the term, awake, but in a so-called hypnotic sleep. In this condition, we may be as fully conscious of the world around us as we are in everyday life, and no intrusive elements may appear of which bystanders in the normal state are unaware. On the other hand, it may equally happen that, in obedience to a hypnotic suggestion, a portion of the external world may disappear, or seem to disappear, for us, and that other objects which do not belong to the external world of other living beings may, in the same way, come into existence for us. These conditions may even, as a result of suggestion, persist after the trance has ceased, reappear *de novo* at a time fixed by the hypnotizer, or first begin to appear long after the trance condition has ceased. To take a few concrete instances, a hypnotizer may, given a sufficiently suggestible subject, impose upon him the idea that a bystander is not really present, and the hypnotic subject will not only not see him, to all appearances, but not even hear him speak.[1] Just as portions of the external world may be, under these circumstances, abolished, the hypnotic subject may likewise take for portions of the external world figures or other objects of sense whose presence is suggested to him.

The important point to notice in the present connexion is that these hallucinations, negative and positive, are not necessarily dependent on the state of consciousness in which the subject is at the moment of the suggestion being realized. I may, for example, suggest to a patient that he will see me six months hence come into his dining room,

---

[1] There is some reason to suppose that the unconsciousness of presence is not absolute. The subject will be discussed in the volume on hypnotism.

say good morning, and disappear up the chimney, and, if he is susceptible, the scene in question will really be enacted, so far as his consciousness at the moment is concerned, though it may happen that he will forget all about it in a short time, just as we frequently forget our dreams, which at the moment of waking seemed vivid enough.

Forgetfulness is a common phenomenon, too common in fact, and it has, in general, no importance for the subject under discussion. The rapid and complete forgetfulness, however, of the incidents of the hypnotic trance, of the post-hypnotic phenomena, and of the dream world into which we pass or may pass every night, to emerge from it the next morning in the space of a few seconds[1] or less, stands on a different plane. We have here to do with what we may term a split-off portion of consciousness, another example of which is seen in the cases, seldom recorded till towards the last quarter of the nineteenth century, of so-called secondary personality, a milder form of which is seen in the cases not uncommonly reported in the papers, where the memory of the past life has vanished, largely if not completely, but is not replaced by the appearance of another personality to replace the lost one, nor by the assumption of another

[1] Some French experiments on this subject go to show that their duration may be measured by tenths instead of whole seconds.

name; the subject is simply lost and remains so until, by hypnotism or other means, the gap between past life and present consciousness is bridged over.

Now the interesting point about these split-off portions of our consciousness is that their existence does not seem to be confined to the dream state or the hypnotic trance. Indeed, the mere fact that post-hypnotic phenomena of the kind mentioned above, can be produced when the ordinary consciousness is entirely ignorant both of the suggestion and of its fulfilment, is proof positive that this is so in the case of such subjects as are susceptible to this kind of suggestion.

Another illustration of this same point is found in the fact that the sense impressions to which allusion was made at the opening of the chapter, which are too faint, or for other reasons do not rise above the threshold of the ordinary consciousness, may by suitable means be recalled by certain persons, not indeed by the ordinary process of remembering them, but by doing what is irreverently termed "putting the subliminal on tap." To take a few examples, if by means of a suitable arrangement a subject is allowed to catch a glimpse of a word or series of words, letters or numbers, which are, however, exposed for too short a time to permit their meaning to be realized or their order to be recalled, it is nevertheless possible to reproduce them exactly as if the subject had been allowed full leisure to read and memorize them. Given a subject who can write automatically by means of planchette (or simply by holding a pencil between the fingers and allowing the hand to move apparently at random) and the words in question may be written down as if they had been seen or heard with perfect distinctness. A friend of mine was once on a tour in America with a large party which included some automatic writers. One day they resolved to try some experiments. One of these was to place an automatic writer at one end of a car in a room by herself, then came the rest of the party, in the central portion of the car, with instructions to shout at the top of their voices, which they carried out in a way that would effectually drown any human voice even without assistance of the noise of the moving train; then, at the other end of the car to the automatic writer, came the experimenter; he had provided himself with a book which he read aloud, and the passage selected contained a sufficient number of uncommon words to make it very unlikely that they would be reproduced by a mere coincidence by the automatic writing. At the close of the experiment the passage in question was compared with the automatic script, and sufficient correspondence was discovered to establish beyond question the fact that the writing was not independent of the selected passage, of which, it is needless to say, the writer had been carefully kept in ignorance.

In the same way, facts which have come under our eyes without reaching our minds may be reproduced. Thus there is the oft-quoted case of the lady who held in front of her face, to shield it from the fire, a copy of the *Times*. A few hours later she looked into a crystal and was surprised to read there the announcement of a death which was subsequently found to be contained in the obituary column.

The whole of this fascinating subject of the subliminal has been studied in great detail in the *Proc. S.P.R.*, by F. W. H Myers, and in a more condensed form in his work on *Human Personality*. For further details we must refer inquirers to these works pending the appearance of other volumes in the present series.

The importance of the subliminal for our present purpose is twofold. In the first place, it is from the subliminal, the portion of our consciousness " below the threshold," or perhaps better " beyond the threshold," that thoughts and pictures arise, as we shall see more in detail in the next chapter.

It is on the analysis of the content of these impressions, mental and sensory, and of the corresponding motor automatisms, and on the comparison of

the results with the ideas present in the mind of
another person or persons, that the case for telepathy rests. The person who is endeavouring
to transfer thoughts or impressions is termed the
agent, the receiver is called the percipient.

In the second place, there is reason to suppose
that the *primâ facie* telepathic impressions, the
impressions communicated by other means than
ordinary sensory methods, depend for their communication in some way on the subliminal consciousness. How this happens we cannot of course
say, and the hyper-sensitiveness of the subliminal, of
which a few illustrations have been given above,
must, of course, put us on our guard against possible
errors of observation. For it must be noted that
we are, as a rule, unaware of how such sub-conscious
impressions reach us (see *Proc. S.P.R.* iv. 532;
Journ. S.P.R. i. 84; and Mrs. Verrall's remarks on
the same subject in *Proc. S.P.R.* vii. 193). As
an example of the importance of this subliminal
communication, if we may so term it without
prejudging the case, may be mentioned the cases
given on pp. 28 and 81.

The interest of the subliminal for us is, however,
not entirely exhausted by these two points. Not
only shall we have occasion to deal with evidence
drawn from dreams, which constitute, as we have
seen, a common form of split-off consciousness,

but we shall have occasion to refer in some detail
to trance phenomena. A person who falls into
trance spontaneously is, in many respects, in a
similar position to a hypnotized subject. There
is unconsciousness of the events of the trance on
awakening, and there is the existence of an apparently normally constituted personality or personal-
ties, who usually claim to be the spirits of deceased
relatives, or other dead persons, who take advantage
of the absence of the medium's spirit to take possession of her body and communicate with this ter-
restrial sphere again. As to the evidence in support
of this claim, nothing need be said in the present
volume. All that is necessary here is to make clear
what happens in the trance.

These trance personalities manifest themselves
in much the same way as the ordinary subliminal,
and there can be no possible doubt that they are,
in most cases, the result of a sort of dramatic instinct
on the part of the human subliminal, which leads
it to dress itself up in a way that it hopes will be
interesting to its auditors. They communicate
sometimes by word of mouth, sometimes by automatic writing, sometimes by both simultaneously,
sometimes even by speech, by ordinary right hand
writing and by mirror writing produced by the
left hand, all at the same time, the subjects of the
three communications being absolutely distinct.

The subject of clairvoyance is not directly connected with that of telepathy, but inasmuch as it would throw some doubt, if proved to exist, on the evidence for telepathy or rather on the interpretation of it, we cannot pass over it here. Clairvoyance is a term used in a variety of meanings, but we are here concerned only with clairvoyance proper, or lucidity, that is to say with the perception of objects directly without the intervention of the ordinary nervous processes. The evidence for any such faculty is very slight and the possibilities of mal-experimentation so large that it would hardly be worth discussing were it not that one of the chief experimenters has been Professor Richet, whose records are usually so ample as to permit us to form an opinion as to the precautions taken to obviate false results.

The first series of experiments was made by M. Richet in the winter of 1887-1888 with a number of diagrams, the nature of which was unknown to any person present, shut up in opaque envelopes, which were only opened after the guess had been made. It is true that in a certain number of cases Professor Richet had been himself the draughtsman; after drawing the diagrams he had put them away and was, so far as he knew, absolutely unaware of their nature. But it is clear that these trials must be eliminated; for it is impossible to say that some part of his mind was not cognisant of their nature—the subliminal has a marvellous memory—consequently it cannot be affirmed that the experiments in which these were used do not, so far as they are successful, point to telepathy rather than clairvoyance. Of the forty-one diagrams which he publishes as being whole or partial successes, only two are of this nature; the remaining thirty-nine were drawn by a personal friend of M. Richet's, sent to him, and utilised unopened.

Of the experiments tried under these conditions, about 26 per cent. were, according to M. Richet's estimate, more or less successful. I have noted seven as being particularly close; some of these I reproduce (Pl. I.). In order to test the possibilities of chance coincidence, a series of guesses, amounting in all to over 5,000, were made and the proportion of successes calculated; they amounted to between 3 per cent. and 4 per cent. The difference is therefore sufficiently marked. It must not, however, be forgotten that, in the experiments proper, the whole series amounted to only 180, a number which may give results differing very widely from the average of a larger number of trials. On the other hand, even here, it is impossible to say that telepathy was altogether excluded. M. Richet does not indeed consider this possibility, which is at best very remote. It cannot, however, be overlooked that

[PLATE I.

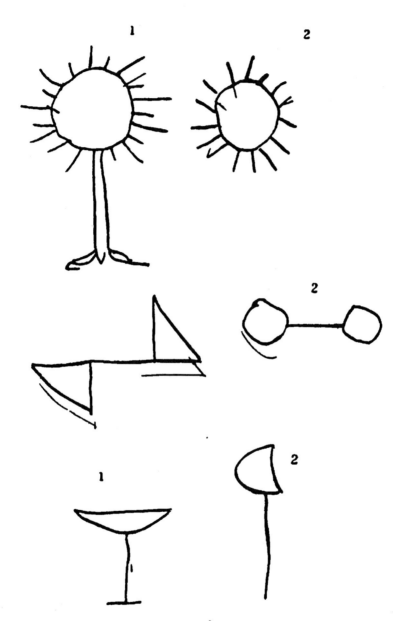

PROF. RICHET'S EXPERIMENTS.

1. DIAGRAMS.   2. REPRODUCTIONS.

[Reduced to one-half.]

a human being was conscious of the contents of the envelopes. That this knowledge should be communicated to M. Richet, in the absence of the person in whose mind the knowledge was, is highly improbable, and the telepathic processes demanded by such an hypothesis are complicated in the extreme. We are, however, not entitled to exclude any hypothesis merely on the ground that it seems to us improbable. Consequently the experiments in question do not seem to be above criticism.

More satisfactory were the conditions in another series tried by Professor Richet in the summer and autumn of 1888. The subject on whom the experiments were tried was one whose name will be quoted in connexion with experiments to be dealt with subsequently—Léonie B. She was hypnotized by the experimenter and kept in the trance state on some occasions from 8 p.m. till 6 a.m., during the whole of which time Professor Richet sat by her. The objects used were cards, drawn from a mixture of ten packets of fifty-two cards each. No card was used a second time.

In order to prevent the subject from seeing the card before it was placed in the envelope, Professor Richet drew it at a distance of sixteen feet from her; in addition she had her back turned and the light was low. The card was drawn and placed as rapidly as possible in a so-called opaque envelope, gummed down and given to the medium. During the experiment, which sometimes lasted for two or three hours, Professor Richet, as may be imagined, sometimes took his eyes off the subject, but never for long enough to permit of any manipulation of the envelope, much less of the precise procedure necessary to open and reclose it without leaving any trace of the operation.

Léonie's procedure was as follows. Taking the envelope in her hands she held it between them and drew on a sheet of paper diagrams of the various suits; then she counted on her fingers to ascertain the number of the pips, the process being repeated *ad nauseam,* till she finally made up her mind. There is no reason whatever to question the good faith of Léonie, as a general rule, but we cannot assume the good faith of hypnotized or any other subjects, when it is possible to conduct the experiments otherwise, without by so doing weakening their evidential character. It is therefore unfortunate that, in these laborious and wearisome experiments, Professor Richet not only allowed Léonie to open the envelope herself on some occasions, but even omitted to note on what occasions she did so. At the same time we can hardly suppose that she was prepared with a card, to which she made her guess correspond. For in the first place it is very unlikely that she would have delayed her answer so long. In the second place there is no reason to suppose that she possessed the conjuring ability necessary to palm off a secreted card and replace the card in the envelope by it, and this at a distance of about a foot from a person who was observing her closely. As a rule, the card was enclosed in one envelope which, although practically opaque so far as transmitted light was concerned, was not entirely so for reflected light. Léonie does not appear, however, to have scrutinized it in a way that suggested that she availed herself of this circumstance; she was, moreover, in a dim light until she made her guess and approached Professor Richet, at the end of the trial, to show him that the envelope was intact, and it was necessary for the light to be strong—full sunshine or a powerful lamp—for anything to be detected in an ordinary way. Moreover, during the last twenty-two trials there was a second envelope, and we may assume that this was sufficient to prevent anything in the way of ordinary vision from giving information as to the card. Yet in four out of the twenty-two trials the card was correctly named.

In all, out of sixty-eight trials twelve cards were named by Léonie, the probability being that she would guess one or two, if no cause other than " chance " operated. The number of suits guessed was thirty-six against a probable seventeen.

When we look at the experiments in detail, the probability of some unrecognized cause being in operation is seen to be enormous.   In the sixty-eight trials a full description of the card was offered only seventeen times; in two cases the description was incomplete; out of the remaining fifteen cards twelve were rightly named, and in the three other cases king of hearts was named for ten of hearts, knave of spades for knave of hearts and queen of diamonds for queen of hearts.

A further series of experiments was tried in which the errors above alluded to were avoided. The results were, however, much less striking.   At the same time there was evidence of a power to select the court cards, seven out of nine named cards being correct.

On the whole it can hardly be said that the experiments go very far to prove anything of the nature of clairvoyance.   Indeed it may be said that in the present state of our knowledge of X-rays, and other waves, we can not be certain that they are imperceptible to the hyperæsthetic. The experiences with N-rays in fact seem to point to considerable variation in this respect in human vision, unless indeed we prefer to take the view that the supposed rays are a product of the imagination and have no objective existence.   Rays of some sort may have given information as to the card in the envelope.

It is equally impossible to be certain that hyperæsthesia of touch would not enable the medium to detect the very slight differences of elevation which must be present, especially in court cards. On the whole, therefore, the value of the experiments of Professor Richet, so far as regards clairvoyance, must be regarded as small.

The same remark applies to experiments in guessing the numbers and suits of cards, and details of some experiments in this by Mrs. Verrall will be found in *Proc. S.P.R.,* vii. 174, *sq.* Mrs. Verrall, who is a most careful experimenter, did not, it should be noted, regard them as having any bearing on the question of clairvoyance, for the simple reason that the subject was, in all cases, able to see the card, if indeed she did not actually draw it. The same is true of a striking series of experiments by Mr. Y., given at the end of Mrs. Verrall's paper. Bearing in mind the already mentioned long memory of the subliminal, together with a possible hyperæsthesia, which is certainly present in some cases, we see that there is no ground for assuming that any but the ordinary operation of the senses, ordinary that is, in respect of species, though extraordinary in respect of practical efficiency, is needed to explain the results.

At the same time, probable though this explanation be, we are bound to recognize that, both in these cases and in the experiments of M. Richet, the possibility of what we have termed clairvoyance has not been excluded, cannot in fact be excluded. It would be of the highest interest if some one who finds him or herself possessed of this power of guessing cards would try a series of experiments specially directed towards elucidating the question of the *modus operandi*.

When we come to deal with certain of the experiments in detail, it will be seen that there is an extraordinary difference between the results attained when the agent and percipient are in the same room and those reached when they are in different rooms. It is of course far more probable that some simpler cause is at work—the nature of which will be suggested when the experiments in question are reached. At the same time it is well to bear in mind that our knowledge of the human mind is very limited and that much of the evidence for telepathy at close quarters might in reality point in another direction.

CHAPTER IV

How we become aware of subliminal ideas—Mental impressions—Visions and hallucinations—Automatic writing

WE have seen in the last chapter that some impressions, too faint to enter our consciousness in the ordinary way, are relegated to the subliminal region of our minds and perhaps stick there, if the subliminal is not " put on tap " in some way. On the other hand, they may slowly emerge into our ordinary consciousness, and we become aware of them by a roundabout route. It happens probably to most people that in walking along the street they hear words the meaning of which they do not appreciate. Especially if they have been living abroad and are familiar with a foreign language does it happen that sentences are heard as meaningless collections of syllables which afterwards straighten themselves out and become intelligible, although the hearer may have been in doubt as to what language they were in and have looked for a clue in the wrong direction.

It has been indicated that there is some ground for supposing that subliminal ideas are specially

important in experiments which go to prove the
existence of telepathy.   In the present chapter we
shall survey some of the methods by which the
subject may either become directly aware of these
subliminal ideas or may so externalize them as to
bring them to the notice at once of bystanders and
of themselves.   These methods are three in number.
The first two result in the subject alone becoming
aware of the images or ideas.   They are respectively
mental impressions and sensory automatisms.

It is unnecessary to deal at length with mental
impressions.   Every one is aware that ideas come
into the mind without our being at the moment
conscious of their origin.   Knowledge arrived at
by means of the ordinary senses, as the experiments of M. Bergson prove (*Rev. Phil.* 1886, p.
127), may enter our consciousness without our being aware of how it got there.   Or, to take another
example, we endeavour in vain to recall a name or
a word and finally give up the attempt.   In a few
minutes, it frequently happens, the desired name
or word comes into our mind without any conscious
effort.

It is clearly immaterial how the idea which rises
to the surface reached the brain of the subject,
whether by ordinary perceptive processes or by
some other method.   If there is such a way of
learning facts or getting impressions as that which

is designated telepathy, these facts or impressions
may manifest themselves in the consciousness of
the percipient in just the same way as any other ideas
originally confined to the subliminal region.

Our second class is known to psychologists as
sensory automatisms. It includes such phenomena
as crystal visions, hallucinations, pseudo-hallucina-
tions and mental images, and, finally, dreams.

When we look at an object, especially a bright
object, and then close our eyes, we commonly see
what is termed an " after-image." With these and
ordinary sense perceptions we have nothing to do.

MENTAL IMAGES

Many people are able at will to call up before their
mind's eye the picture of an object or a scene, which
they have once beheld, with all the vividness with
which they are commonly seen in a dream. Others,
among whom I am included, are unable to visualize,
as it is technically termed, or are only able to do so
imperfectly, possibly only at intervals. So far as
I am aware, I have only once been able to visualize
at will during my ordinary waking moments, and
then the object which I called up before me was
no more inspiring than an ordinary cane-bottomed
chair. Just as, as far as we can see, the life of the
dog must be very largely made up of sensations
of smell, and his recollections present themselves

to him in the form of smells and possibly tastes, so the recollections of the visualizer seem to present themselves in the form of mental pictures. But mental pictures also flow across the visual field without their being consciously called up, and a subliminal idea which is the result of a telepathic message may manifest itself in the form of a mental image. An interesting experiment with this form of perception will be found on p. 148.

These mental pictures are clearly recognized as things of the mind. In technical language they are not externalized. In addition to these non-externalized cases, we have several distinct classes of visual perceptions, which appear to be located among the actual surroundings of the percipient and consequently must count as externalized. It must be understood that there is no hard and fast line of demarcation however. Between the mental images and the externalized vision or hallucination come a class of phenomena which are termed *illusions hypnagogiques*. Before one is wholly asleep or wholly awake, a half dream state seems to super-vene in some persons, which is characterized by the appearance of pictures, frequently faces, before their eyes, which may be closed or not. In some people they are very rare; I have, for example, only once seen anything of the sort—a weird procession of eyes, lions' eyes, crocodiles' eyes, snakes' eyes, an interminable series, due to no cause, mental or physical, that I could trace. In others again they seem to be a normal sign of approaching sleep. They are more than mere memory images, but yet not fully externalized.

VISIONS

Coming now to the next class, that of externalized pictures, we have first of all visions, that is to say, pictures which appear to occupy a place among the surroundings of the percipient, but not to be of them. As an example of this class we may quote a case published some ten years ago in the Report of the International Census on Hallucinations. A lady, Mrs. B., was in Italy and engaged in no more exciting occupation than giving her children their dinner. She was just standing over a tureen of milk and maccaroni, when she happened to look at the wall in front of her and saw it apparently open. The scene that presented itself to her was a bedroom in a house that was very familiar to her; on the bed lay the corpse of her mother with flowers on her breast. It subsequently turned out that the mother had died six days before and been buried at the time Mrs. B. saw the vision. She had not been informed of her mother's death, owing to the fact that she had quarrelled with her family and left England without giving an address.

Another class of visions is the kind which is seen

in crystals, bright surfaces, water, ink, or, which
brings it very near the *illusions hypnagogiques,* in
black boxes or other dark spaces. These visions
are sometimes so extraordinarily life-like, that I have
seen people who experienced them for the first
time thoroughly puzzled and suspicious of some
trick by which living pictures were in some way
produced in the crystal.

HALLUCINATIONS

Besides visions, our externalized pictures may
also take the form of hallucinations. As a technical
term hallucination simply means an object of sense
perception or percept which is not due to any external cause, though it seems to be so due and can
only be recognized as lacking the external cause with
which we associate it when we come to analyse it.
The term hallucination has unpleasant associations
for some people and suggests ideas of delirium tre-
mens, lunacy, and all manner of objectionable things.
It must be remembered that, as a technical term
of psychical research, it has no necessary connexion
with anything morbid. No one will, for example,
be alarmed because he happens to dream; but a dream
is, technically, an hallucination and a particularly
good example of one, as we shall see in a few moments. In our dreams we form part of an hallucinatory picture, talk to the hallucinatory person-

ages whom we have conjured up, move about in the hallucinatory scenery, and so on. In fact, it is only rarely that we recognize before awakening that it is a dream.

The hallucinations of our waking moments are much rarer than those of sleep, and consequently far more likely to make an impression. At the same time, the fact that we are awake makes it far easier to remember and note down the exact details. This form of hallucination is therefore particularly valuable evidentially. In waking hallucinations it usually happens that only a single figure or portion of the scene is hallucinatory, and herein lies its chief difference from the dream. The dream figures, for such they may be called, which we see during our waking moments, move about in our ordinary surroundings and appear to form part of them. In fact, it may be that only on reflection do we discover that they are dream figures. The best example of this class of hallucinations is the common ghost, and by that I mean, not the ghost of Christmas stories, which clanks chains and looks with mournful and despairing eyes at you; real ghosts are far too unconscious of their surroundings[1] to do anything

[1] I do not mean to imply that in the case of the real ghost there is anything of the nature of the material or immaterial being occupying the space where the figure is seen. The series will include a volume on ghosts, in which the matter will be fully discussed.

rational as a rule; the ghost of which you hear when you get a story at first hand is an object that is frequently in many respects like a living person, but is discovered to differ from the ordinary human being by a trick that it has of disappearing in an unaccountable way, or perhaps of fading away before your eyes.

ILLUSIONS

For the sake of completeness, we may mention illusions. Illusions differ from hallucinations in that they are interpretations of real objects and not wholly the work of the mind. How far any hallucinations, except dreams, come under this category it is hard to say. Probably many that eventually act in every way independently of the spot at which they were first seen, may have had a so-called *point de repère* in the first instance, round which they formed, just as the crystal vision is often initiated by the specks in the crystal globe.

Examples of most kinds of hallucinations which cannot be discussed in detail here, will be found in the experiments cited in the discussion of the evidence for telepathy.

MOTOR AUTOMATISM

Besides these sensory automatisms just discussed, we shall have to deal with examples of motor automatism. By this is meant an impulse, not proceeding from a conscious volition, which results in the production of writing by means of planchette or otherwise, of table tipping, of the production of movements in the divining rod and of similar phenomena. Just as in sensory automatisms an impulse comes up from some unconscious stratum of our personality that results in an impression being made on our minds which exactly resembles normal sense perception, so in motor automatism an impulse sets in motion the muscles which are usually under the control of the will and produces results which simulate closely or in many cases exactly the results which we are accustomed to regard as due to the exercise of intelligence.

As an example of the intelligence, not to say malice, of planchette, we may quote a true story in which figured a young lady who cherished an affection for a certain young man, whom she was in the habit of meeting on Sunday mornings without the knowledge of her parents. One day the said young lady was asking questions of planchette, which was moving under the hands of another person, her parents being also present. Among other inquiries she wished to know whether it would be fine after church the following day. Instead of giving a straightforward reply, planchette responded to the unspoken thought in her mind, and replied by the single word " George," to the confusion of the questioner and the planchette writer, who was in the secret, but far from wishing to betray it. .

Automatic writing may also be produced in other ways. It is sufficient, in the case of many people, for them to take a pencil between forefinger and thumb and put a sheet of paper beneath. If they then take a book or otherwise divert their attention from the motions of their hand, it will probably be found to trace scrawls on the paper. These scrawls develop in a certain number of cases into an intelligible script, which differs indeed very widely from the ordinary handwriting of the individual, but is perfectly coherent at times, though not always easy to read.

Although none of the experiments dealt with below are concerned with table tipping, it may be mentioned here, for the sake of completeness in our brief survey in the various modes of automatic expression with which psychical research has to deal. Similarly, we may mention without discussing the performances of water diviners. Whatever the explanation of water divining, it is certain that it is a perfectly genuine gift, which is not confined to those who make a living by it, but shared by many respectable and even distinguished members of society.

Another example, possibly, of motor automatism is to be found in the so-called willing game, though here it is always possible that the movement is more voluntary and dependent rather on the evocation of a picture of the position in which a hidden object has to be sought or other sensory idea, rather than upon motor automatism proper. With technicalities of this sort, however, we are little concerned, the less so as no examples of the willing game are quoted in the present volume, for reasons that will be explained below.

We have now surveyed the field with which we have to deal, that is to say, we have briefly glanced at the various methods by which an idea, *primâ facie* telepathic, is found to emerge into consciousness. We may now proceed to the discussion of the experiments in detail.

CHAPTER V

Historical—The Magnetizers—Spiritualism—The Newnham experiments—Experiments by Mr. Malcolm Guthrie, Professor Sidgwick and others.

As the present work does not treat of thought transference in general, I will not attempt to give in detail the history of the idea, but only to discuss some of the already published experimental evidence and supplement it by experiments conducted by myself. It may, however, be interesting to recall briefly some facts which, if their significance had been seen, would have led to an earlier development of interest in the subject, the appearance of which, as a branch of investigation, does not in fact date further back than 1876, when it was brought to the notice of the British Association by Professor W. F. Barrett, F.R.S., President of the Society for Psychical Research at the time when these words were written.

Hypnotism has now been studied for a good deal more than a hundred years. As far back as the twenties of the nineteenth century Puysegur and other French magnetizers detected in their subjects what was known to a later generation of English observers as " community of sensation," and the facts were investigated by a commission, appointed by the French Academy, which sat for no less than five years before presenting a report in 1831, and affirmed the reality of " l'action à distance." With a truly admirable regard for the " facts " of science, they resolved not to publish the report, because, if the majority of the statements were correct, one half of physiology would go by the board, and the dissemination of such knowledge would have been dangerous.

How far this attitude led to the question being ignored it is difficult to say.   Perhaps, had the French Academy taken a broader view of " science " and faced the possibility of a reconstruction of hypotheses to make them suit the facts instead of cutting their facts to fit their hypotheses, telepathy might have been a subject of general interest fifty years earlier, and the investigation might have done much to induce men of science to take up " occult " questions generally, and to check the growth of spiritualism by suggesting that the spiritistic interpretation of certain facts was incorrect. The English observations failed to excite attention from a rather different cause. On the one hand, the medical side of hypnotism was mainly to the fore, on the other hand, the interest in its psychical side was choked, to a large extent, by the ranker vegetation of spiritualism, which traces its origin to the Rochester rappings of 1848. Morin, *Du Magnetisme* (Paris, 1860), affirms the existence of thought transference, but means no more than the interpretation of a somnambulist of the thoughts of a person by means of a study of his features, unconscious though it may be.

To one acute observer, however, if to no more, the idea of telepathy presented itself as an explanation of spiritualistic marvels. Writing in the *Spectator* of January 30, 1869, Mr., now Sir James, Knowles, editor of the *Nineteenth Century,* suggested brain waves as the explanation of death wraiths,[1] of so-called clairvoyance, and of other facts now more familiar to us than they were in those days. The idea had occurred to him as much as eighteen years earlier in 1851, in connexion with hypnotic experiments, and we thus have a writer linking the English magnetists with the Society for Psychical Research and its immediate predecessors.

[1] The idea was, of course, not entirely new. Cf. Walton's *Life of Donne*, pp. 24, 25. The suggested explanation of the apparition of Mrs. Donne seems to be that it had something to do with brain waves. The author regards the case as analogous to that of two lutes, both of which vibrate when one is struck.

The same theory of spiritualistic manifestations was put forward, apparently independently, by Mr. H. M. Andrew in the first number of the *Melbourne Review,* issued in January, 1875, as a result of various experiments tried in 1873 or 1874, with a view of showing that the knowledge of the spiritualistic medium emanated from the brain of the sitter.

Six months earlier, in August, 1875, Dr. Mcgraw had expressed the opinion, in the *Detroit Review of Medicine,* that features in the willing game seemed to hint at the possibility of one man's nervous system being used by the active will of another to accomplish certain simple movements.

The real protagonist of psychical research in the world of science was, as has already been mentioned, Professor Barrett. His paper of 1876 dealt mainly with the phenomena manifested by hypnotized subjects whom he selected from among the children of a village in Westmeath, but the first published experiments date back to the year 1871 and were carried out by the Rev. P. H. Newnham and his wife. The *modus operandi* was as follows: Mrs. Newnham sat at a low table in a low chair, leaning backwards; her husband sat about eight feet distant at a rather high table, with his back towards Mrs. Newnham, who, as a rule, kept her eyes shut; he wrote down questions,

of the wording and purport of which Mrs. Newnham was absolutely unaware, and which she, in many
cases, answered successfully by means of planchette,
even when the facts given in her answer were not
and never had been known to her. The questions
were not communicated to Mrs. Newnham when an
evasive or other answer was returned which
necessitated further questions, nor even the
general subject to which they alluded. The
answers were occasionally illegible and sometimes
irrelevant, but in the latter case it was generally
found that they had reference to a previous question
which had not been fully dealt with. It was
possible to explain most of the few wrong answers
by reference to the circumstances of the moment,
and in nearly every case the purport of the question
seems to have been understood. A statistical
analysis of the results being impossible, owing to the
nature of many of the answers, it is unnecessary to
deal at length with the full series of 309 questions,
details of which will be found in a paper on Automatic Writing by the late F. W. H. Myers.[1] From
the point of view of evidence it is important to
notice that, assuming the good faith of the experimenters, which there is absolutely no reason to
doubt, the results having been noted in a diary
obviously not intended for publication and only

[1] *Proc. S.P.R.,* iii. 6-23.

made known eleven years after the event, the conditions were remarkably good. It may, of course, be argued that the minds of husband and wife are apt to move in similar grooves, but it must be remembered that with the exception of eight months in 1871 Mrs. Newnham never manifested the power of answering her husband's unspoken thoughts. The same remark applies, though with less force, to the criticism that Mrs. Newnham may have become aware of the purport of the questions, by subconscious interpretation, by the sounds produced by the pencil in writing the questions. But, apart from the improbability of this, the correct answers of the facts of which Mrs. Newnham had no knowledge, absolutely negative this explanation in some cases and any hypothesis must of course cover the whole of the facts.

From 1881 onwards many series of experiments were made, details of which will be found in the publications of the *S.P.R.*[1] I will not do more than quote some of the more important experiments and give statistical abstracts of those in which the conditions seem satisfactory.

An important contribution to the subject was made by Mr. Malcolm Guthrie's experiments in

[1] *Proc. S.P.R.* vols i. to xii.; *Journal S.P.R.* vols i. to x., etc. A convenient résumé is given by Mr. Podmore in *Apparitions and Thought Transference*, pp. 18–143.

transference of tastes and pains. In the case of tastes, fifteen experiments[1] were tried on September 5, 1883, the agents being Mr. Guthrie, Mr. Edmund Gurney and Mr. Myers. The percipients were two ladies, Miss Edwards, who on the occasion in question was less sensitive than usual owing to a sore throat, and Miss Relph. In order to prevent errors arising from a possible smell given off by the substances, they were kept outside the room in which the percipients were, and in a dark lobby, so that the agents selected them at random and one investigator was often unaware of what the others took. The results are sufficiently striking to be worth giving in detail.—

No. of experi- ment.	Agents.	Perci- pient.	Substance.	Answer.
1.	E.G. & M[2]	E	Carbonate of Soda	—
2.	M.G.	R	Carraway Seeds.	"It feels like meal —like a seed loaf —carraway seeds.
3.	E.G. & M.	E	Cloves	Cloves.
4.	E.G. & M.	E	Citric Acid	—
5.	M.G.	R	Citric Acid	Salt.
6.	E.G. & M.	E	Liquorice	Cloves.
7.	M.G.	R	Cloves	Cinnamon.
8.	E.G. & M.	E	Acid Jujube	Pear drop.

[1] Proc. S.P.R. ii. 3, sq.

[2] E.G.—Edmund Gurney; M.—Myers; M.G.—Malcolm Guthrie. The agent is the sender of the presumed telepathic message, the percipient the receiver of the same.

No. of experiment.	Agents.	Perci-pient.	Substance.	Answer.
9.	M.G.	R	Acid Jujube.	Something hard which is giving way—acid jujube.
10.	E.G. & M.	E	Candied Ginger	Something sweet and hot.
11.	M.G.	R	Candied Ginger.	Almond toffy. [M.G. did not realize at once that he had ginger.]
12.	E.G. & M.	E	Home made Noyau Salt.	
13.	M.G.	R	Home made Noyau Port Wine.	
14.	E.G. & M.	E	Bitter Aloes	—
15.	M.G.	R	Bitter Aloes	—

Excluding the cases where nothing was felt, E. got 1 completely right and 3 nearly right out of 6 trials; R. got 2 completely right and 2 nearly right out of the same number, making 3 completely rights and 5 approximations out of 12 trials. The total number of substances used was about 20; assuming that as a result of previous trials the percipients were aware of this, we find that the probability of their guessing right was 5 in 100; they actually succeeded 5 times as often, without counting the 42 per cent. of approximations, the precise value of which it is difficult to estimate. The absolute failures, which should have formed 95 per cent. of the answers, were actually only 10 per cent. of them. The good faith of those concerned, an element in the evidence to which I do not propose to allude as a rule, being assumed, the only objection that can be brought against the series, apart from an unfortunate lack of detail in the published reports as to the conditions under which the experiments were carried out, lies in the possibility of the detection of odours by the percipients. But it may be noted that the home made noyau, which is recorded to have been by far the most strong smelling of the substances tried, was guessed by one percipient as salt.

In the summary given by Mr. Guthrie[1] we find that pains were successfully localized without contact in 8 out of 10 guesses, or 66 per cent. in a series where, excluding cases where no impression was got, out of 97 trials of various sorts only 32 answers were correct, or about 33 per cent. In all the three series with contact the successes were forty-four and the approximations 20 out of a total of 82 real trials, or percentages of 54 and 24 with only 22 per cent. of failures. Bearing in mind that the percentage of complete successes under all conditions diminished from 61 in the first series to 37 in the second and 38 in the third, it is remarkable that the pain series without contact in the third series should have shown results superior to those of all the series with contact together or any of them

[1] *Proc. S.P.R.* iii. **427, 428.**

separately. This seems to indicate that in this set of experiments, at any rate, contact had little influence on the results.

In all these cases, however, exact statistical data as 'to the probabilities are excluded by the very nature of the case, save in such instances as the smells, diagrams, pains, etc., from which the selection is made, are known to the percipient. The case is different where the objects to be guessed are cards drawn from a pack or numbers between certain limits. Professor Richet tried a large number of experiments with cards, and he was imitated by members of the S.P.R. and others.[1] In a total of 20,580 trials the suit was named correctly 5,549 times as against a probable number of 5,145 successes, a plus of 404 successes or more than 7 per cent., a discrepancy less considerable indeed than that got by Professor Richet, but more remarkable as being found in experiments eleven times more numerous.

Perhaps the best and most important experiments yet made, both as regards the excellence of the condition and the results attained, are those conducted at Brighton by Professor and Mrs. Sidgwick from 1889 to 1892. In the first series, covering the

[1] *Revue Phil.* 1884, 622–628. The probability that chance alone did not operate in a portion of the series consisting of 1,833 trials was calculated at .99996 (i.e. practically certainty), by Professor F. Y. Edgeworth.

period from July to October, 1889, the percipients, four in all, were hypnotised by Mr. G. A. Smith, who also acted as agent. The objects were counters with the numbers from ten to ninety in raised figures coloured red, the surrounding wood being uncoloured. An elaborate record and analysis of the experiments is given in *Proc. S.P.R.* vi. 128-170, to which reference must be made by those who wish to go into details. The amount of success varied to a singular extent, a point that on the whole seems to tell in favour of the telepathic explanation, for any cause of error may be assumed to have operated under similar conditions in a degree approximately equal. Taking the percipients separately, we find that with agent and percipient in the same room, 345 trials were made with P, and 263 with T; with agent and percipient in different rooms, 139 trials were made with P, and 79 with T; in all, 617 under the former and 218 under the latter conditions. Of the former, the digits were given 90 times correctly and 14 times more in reversed order, the most probable number of successes being in each case eight.[1]

On the successful days [2] there were 245 trials and 60 successes (excluding second guesses and 10 cases

[1] The chances of success were 1 in 81. Second guesses are excluded.

[2] When three or more correct guesses were made.

of reversed digits) with P, and 129 trials with 23 successes with T. On other days there were 243 trials in all and only 12 successes. This is, however, considerably above the figure which pure chance, usually termed " expectation," would give.

On the successful days, second guesses and reversed digits being left out of account, there were 133 first digits, and 119 second digits given correctly against an expectation of 46 and 38; on the unsuccessful the numbers were 38 and 32 with expectation 29 and 29. In all, 171 and 151 with expectation 75 and 62.

Of the 139 trials made with P and the agent in different rooms,[1] there was no guess made in 8 cases. In the remaining 131 cases there were 7 complete successes and one case in which the digits were reversed; in 6 cases the first digit was given correctly and in 11 cases the second digit, the expectation being 1 or 2 complete successes, 7 first digits and 6 second.[2] In 71 of these trials Mr. Smith was in the room below, and apparently entirely out of hearing of the percipients. In this series there were 2 successes, the expectation being 1 or 0.

A curious theory was put forward by Lehmann

[1] For details of the place of experiments, see the original reports.

[2] As 0 cannot come first, there is one figure less to choose from.

and Hansen,[1] to account for the results here sum-
marised, and more particularly for those results
which were attained when agent and percipient
were in the same room. These experimenters set
themselves to find out by what means the results
could, under the assigned conditions and assuming
the good faith of the experimenters, have been
attained, and came to the conclusion that unconscious whispering of the numbers was the clue to the
marvel. Accordingly they "whispered unconsciously" in their laboratory for considerable periods
at a time and recorded the successes and failures,
successes being the cases in which the "unconscious"
whisperer, with the aid of a parabolic mirror, transmitted to his fellow experimenter the number which
he had previously selected as the one to be whispered "unconsciously."

The whole thing being prearranged, the term,
"unconscious whispering," seems ill-chosen, and
the meaning would have been better expressed by
"surreptitious whispering," so far as the Lehmann-
Hansen experiments were concerned. Their case
being, however, that the whispering in the Sidgwick
experiments was unconscious and not surreptitious,
they transferred the term "unconscious" to their
own experiments, which had no real relation to

[1] Ueber Unwillkürliches Flüstern, *Phil. Stud.* Bd. 11, Heft,
4, 1895.

the question at issue. Their studies should obviously have been directed to proving that people, who were unaware of the object of the experiment, would frequently, when told to think intently of a number or other word, whisper the word in question, or so far reproduce it by expiratory or inspiratory movements that another person would be guided in his guess to a sufficient extent to influence the results to the extent indicated.

Perhaps the most remarkable feature of the investigation was that, in addition to being concerned with an entirely different set of phenomena to those alleged to have occurred in the Sidgwick experiments, the results were entirely inconclusive. An analysis of the Sidgwick experiments was given, with the idea of proving that auditory transmission was the best explanation of certain errors. But a counter-analysis by Professor Sidgwick [1] showed that errors not explicable on this theory were no less numerous, and that consequently the Lehmann-Hansen hypothesis was not only not proved, but not even proved to be probable. This Professor Lehmann, with a candour that is only too rare, admitted to be the case. [2]

The other Brighton series, carried on by Mrs. Sidgwick and Miss Johnson, at intervals during

[1] *Proc. S.P.R.* xii. 298, *sq.*
[2] *Journ. S.P.R.*

1890-1-2, were mainly of three kinds. In the first the agent and percipient were in different rooms and the objects were, as before, numbers. In 252 trials with Miss B. as percipient there were 27 complete successes, 112 first digits, and 50 second digits right, as against expectation of 3-4, 30 and 25. There were also 8 cases in which the digits, if reversed, would form the correct number, the expectation being here, too, of course, 3-4.

In a series with agent and percipient in the same room the successes were 26 out of 146 trials, the first digits right 53, and the second, 47, as against expectation of 1-2, 16, and 15.

It is important to notice how strongly this tells against any possible transmission by ordinary means. The complete successes were, it is true, more numerous than when the agent was in another room, but so were the right second digits, and the causes which led to the change were not difficult to discover. When the agent and percipient were in different rooms, the guess was not communicated to the agent, who then may have failed to devote special attention to the second digit; this he would however, naturally do, if he were in the same room, and knew that one digit had been correctly guessed or that a guess had been made.

In all these trials in different rooms, the distance between agent and percipient was inconsiderable and varied from 10 to 17 feet. It was indeed sufficient in the opinion of the experimenters to make the words of an ordinary conversation inaudible, but it was considered desirable to try a series in which the distance was sufficient to make auditory indication impossible. Unfortunately, the success in 400 trials was practically *nil*, and for this no sufficient cause could be discovered other than the effect of distance on the imagination by the agent or percipient. This may be a *vera causa* so far as it interferes with the concentration of attention, but how far a concentration of attention is necessary or desirable in either agent or percipient we do not know; consequently this explanation is hardly satisfactory. The complete failure in this series cannot but cast some doubt on the results in those experiments where auditory communication was not impossible, for, as will be seen later, in other cases, distance does not seem to have had an exceptionally disturbing influence on the trials. On the other hand, auditory transmission, exceedingly easy in the case of numbers, is exceedingly difficult in the case of diagrams and pictures, whether we suppose the indications to be given unconsciously or as a result of collusion between agent and percipient. The force of the argument from failure will be much diminished if the same results are found in a series where transference of pictures was aimed at.

Among the other experiments was a series, useless, of course, for exact numerical estimation of the relation of the results to expectation, in which indications, other than verbal suggestion, were apparently impossible, and where, so far as can be seen from the records, verbal suggestion was excluded; it showed an extraordinary disproportion between the results attained when agent and percipient were in the same and in different rooms.[1] In the first case, the successes were 31 out of 71 trials, of which 13 were blanks and resulted in no impression, in the second, the failures were 44 out of 55 trials, the successes 2, and the blanks, 9.[2] It is therefore fairly clear that unless we assume the causes of success to have been different in the two kinds of experiments, it must either be shown that the agent or some person acquainted with the details of the picture gave, either consciously or unconsciously, sufficient indications to guide the percipient, and that these indications, which were not detected by the experimenters whose business it was to do so, were either sufficiently definite to prevent the percipient from starting with a wrong idea and developing it along lines which would result in the failure of the experiment, or were of a character to check a mistaken development and bring the ideas

[1] As to a possible cause of this, see p. 76.
[2] *Proc. S.P.R.* viii. 56.

of the percipient, in the first case erroneous, into line with those of the agent.

The slow emergence of the idea in some of the successful trials and the unpromising fragments from which the final picture, built up from various elements previously seen, was constructed, seem to weigh heavily against the idea of either collusion or unconscious indication. Take for example the fourth experiment with Miss B.,[1] when the subject was a Christy Minstrel with a banjo. The first thing described by her was, " something long, something round in that one—a little cage of some sort— something that looks like a cage; yet there's something like a handle. A can! Oh, it's a can! It's quite clear now." Subsequently she described a hand, a black hand, and then, although the subject had not meanwhile been mentioned, in the course of the next experiment, she went on, " a man, black; he's got something in his hand—an instrument—sort of guitar thing."

It is, of course, possible to argue that conscious collusion may simulate anything, and that consequently we have only to deal with an ingenious mystification. But a sceptic who takes this view would probably find it difficult, under similar conditions, to produce by this means anything equally effective. As regards unconscious indications the

[1] *Proc. S.P.R.* viii., 561.

same holds good, and in this case the additional fact of the circuitous route by which the final result was reached is also in want of explanation. The slow emergence of the correct impression has been so often paralleled in my own experiments, where I am satisfied there was no collusion, I myself being in many cases the agent, and where collusion, and still more unconscious indication implied a so much greater possibility of communicating a picture, or still more a nondescript diagram, difficult to paint in words under any circumstances, than experience seemed to admit, that this explanation does not commend itself to me.

There are, however, two points in which the conditions seem open to criticism. In the first place the picture to be transferred was selected, not drawn at random from a number previously prepared. There was, therefore, a certain scope for the working of association, though it would be unwise to attach great importance to this element. More important is the fact that the agent, in order to maintain the concentration of attention and ensure a due distribution of it over all parts of the picture, was permitted to make a pencil sketch of the picture to be transferred. In the case of a complicated object, this can hardly have affected the result to any great extent, so far as one can see. Still, in view of our ignorance of the limits of hyperæsthesia, possible indications of this sort would have been better avoided. In a series of experiments with cards designed expressly for the purpose of seeing how far the audible indications of the pencil could be interpreted, I found the proportion of successes rose, when the card to be guessed was recorded before, instead of after, the guess.[1]

Numerous other experiments, references to which will be found in the bibliography, were tried in the ten years from 1882 to 1892; and the results were so far conclusive that telepathy was regarded as an established fact, not only by the Society itself, or rather by its individual members, but also by the world at large, so far as daily and, to a large extent, weekly journalism is concerned. This attitude would perhaps have been justified if the same or other experimenters had succeeded in producing a steady flow of experiments with results distinctly above expectation, even if they did not attain the high level of the Brighton series. This was, however, by no means the case, and so long as the Society fails to produce evidence of this nature, so long will the world be justified in a sceptical attitude, and so long can it be said that one of the main objects of the S.P.R. remains unattained.

[1] As the recorder was also the agent, it is possible that the mere act of writing down the card facilitated thought transference. I was unable to make a sufficiently extended series to form an opinion on the point.

CHAPTER VI

Experiments at a distance—Transference of images
—Telepathic hallucinations

ALTHOUGH comparatively little evidence has been
published, it would not be fair to pass over the trials
at a distance. It is manifestly impossible to object
to the conditions under which such experiments are
tried, provided the diagrams are sufficiently varied
and selected at random. The experiments of the
Rev. A. Glardon, Miss Despard, and others are
worthy of note and seem difficult to explain by any
theory of chance coincidence. It should, however,
not be forgotten that the series were comparatively
short—a defect that could be readily repaired, if
it were once realized that the evidence for telepathy
is far from being complete, while the laws, if any,
that govern its manifestations, and the mode in
which ideas are transmitted, are hidden in the
deepest mystery.

Miss Despard tried her experiments in the summer
of 1892 with a friend of hers, Miss Campbell, with
whom she had tried a successful series of experiments at close quarters a few months previously. The

conditions of the experiment were recorded in writing beforehand; after the trial the percipient recorded her impression at once and before hearing from the agent. The first experiment was as follows :—[1]

No. 1.   *June 22, 1892.*

Arranged that R. C. Despard should, when at the School of Medicine in Handel Street, W.C., between the hours of 11.50 and 11.55, fix her attention on some object which Miss Campbell, at 77, Chesterton Road, W., is by thought transference to discover.

PERCIPIENT'S ACCOUNT.

Owing to an unexpected delay, instead of being quietly at home at 11.50 a.m., I was waiting for my train at Baker Street, and as just at that time trains were moving away from both platforms and there was the usual bustle going on, I thought it hopeless to try on my part; but just while I was thinking this I felt a sort of mental pull-up, which made me feel sure that Miss Despard was fixing *her* attention, and directly after I felt " my compasses—no, scalpel," seemed to see a flash of light as if on bright steel, and I thought of two scalpels, first with their points together and then folding together into one; just then my train came up.

I write this down before having seen Miss Despard,

---

[1] Podmore, *Apparitions*, p. 127.

so am still in ignorance whether I am correct in my surmise, but, as I know what Miss Despard would probably be doing at ten minutes to twelve, I feel that my knowledge may have suggested the thought to me, though this idea did not occur to me until just this minute, as I have written it down.

C. M. CAMPBELL.

77, CHESTERTON ROAD, W.

AGENT'S ACCOUNT.

At ten minutes to twelve I concentrated my mind on an object that happened to be in front of me at the time—two scalpels, crossed, with their points together; but in about five minutes, as it occurred to me that the knowledge I was at the School of Medicine might suggest a similar idea to Miss Campbell, I tried to bring up a country scene, of a brook running through a field .with a patch of yellow marsh marigolds in the foreground. This second idea made no impression on Miss Campbell —perhaps owing to the bustle around her at the time.

R. C. DESPARD.

No. 2.   *October 25, 1892.*

At 3.30 p.m. R. C. Despard is to fix her attention on some object, and C. M. Campbell, being in a different part of London, is by thought transference to find out what the object is.

PERCIPIENT'S ACCOUNT.

At 3.30 I was at home at 77, Chesterton Road, North Kensington, alone in my room.

First my attention seemed to flit from one object to another, while nothing definite stood out, but soon I saw a pair of gloves, which became more definitely distinct till they appeared as a pair of baggy tan-coloured kid gloves, certainly a size larger than worn by either R.C.D. or myself, and not quite like any of ours in colour. After this I saw a train going out of a station (I had just returned from seeing some one off at Victoria), almost obliterated by a picture of a bridge over a small river, but I felt that I was consciously thinking and left off the experiment, being unable to clear my mind sufficiently of outside things.

AGENT'S ACCOUNT.

At 3.30 on October 25 I was at 30, Handel Street, Brunswick Square, W.C. C.M.C. and myself had arranged beforehand to make an experiment in thought transference at that hour, I to try to transfer some object to her mind, the nature of which was left entirely unspecified. I picked up a pair of rather old tan-coloured gloves—purposely not taking a pair of my own—and tried for about five minutes to concentrate my attention on them and the wish to transfer an impression of them to

C.M.C.'s mind.   After this I fixed my attention on
a window, but felt my mind getting tired, and
therefore rather disturbed by the constant sound
of omnibuses and waggons passing the open window.

R. C. DESPARD.

October 25, 1892.

A month later Miss Campbell wrote, giving some
further details as follows: " With regard to the
distant experiments, the notes sent to you were the
only ones made.   In the first experiment (scalpels),
I wrote the account before Miss Despard's return,
and when Miss Despard returned, before seeing
what I had written, she told me what she had
thought of, and almost directly wrote it down.

" In the second experiment (gloves) I was just
going to write my account when Miss Despard
returned home, and she asked me at once, ' Well,
what did you think of ? '   I told her a pair of tan
gloves, then sat down and wrote my account, and
when she had read it through, she said, ' Yes, you
have exactly described Miss M.'s gloves, which I
was then holding while I fixed my attention on
them,' and then she wrote her account."

As has been pointed out above, these experiments
are too few in number to give much security against
chance successes.   Moreover, as Miss Campbell
points out, the object in the first case was by no

means above suspicion. The trials are also open to some objection on the ground that the notes of the experiments were not made at the earliest possible moment. With feminine caution, the experimenters refrained from recording their own share until they had some assurance that the trial had not been a failure. It is very probable that this little peculiarity made absolutely no difference to the record; but where so much depended upon the form and the words, it would have been wiser to write down all the facts worthy of being recorded as soon as the experiment was finished. Addenda can readily be made and noted as such. It need hardly be said that the objection to record failures, if this was the real reason for the procedure under discussion, is fatal to the value of the experiments; where there is any reason to suppose that only successful trials are recorded, we have no data for estimating the proportion of failures. In the present case, however, the two experiments quoted seem to have been the only ones made at a distance.

In the same year, Mr. Kirk and Miss G., who had two years previously tried a series of twenty-two with but moderate success, renewed their attempts, and out of the seven experiments tried, two were of a distinctly striking character.[1] The fourth trial of the series was on May 1. Miss G.'s im-

[1] Podmore, *loc. cit.* p. 133.

pressions were recorded in part the same night, in part the following morning before she saw Mr. Kirk. She saw " a broken circle, then only faint patches of light, not cloudlike but flat, which alternated with vertical streaks of pale light." This part of her record, written on the same evening, seems to refer to the first part of Mr. Kirk's experiment. Later she had, " soon after lying down last night, a rapid but most realistic glimpse of Mr. Kirk leaning against his dining-room mantelpiece; the room seemed brightly lighted, and he looked rather bothered, and just as I saw him he appeared to say, ' Doctor,[1] I haven't got my pipe.' This seemed to me very absurd, the more so as I do not know whether Mr. Kirk ever smoked a pipe. I see him occasionally with a cigar or cigarette, but cannot remember ever having seen him with a pipe; if I have, it must have been years ago. I do not know whether my eyes were open or closed, but the vividness of the impression quite startled me. This occurred just after the expiration of time appointed for experiment (10.45-11.15)."

After seeing this report, Mr. Kirk, who of course did not record at the time what he supposed to have had no connexion with his experiment, wrote as follows: " The fact that I had another experiment

[1] A familiar name given to Miss G. by Mr. Kirk and his wife.

to make [i.e. after the trial with Miss G.] enables me to trace minutely my actions before beginning it. Immediately the time had expired with Miss G. I got up [from the low chair] and rapidly lit the gas and three pieces of candle, which I had ready in the cardboard box cover, to illuminate the diagram. The room was therefore brilliantly lighted. I now rested with my right shoulder against the mantelpiece, with my face towards Miss G. [i.e. in the direction in which she was, for she was not in the same house], but with my eyes bent on the carpet. In this position I thought intensely of myself and the whole room, and feeling really anxious to make a success, for at least six minutes. By this time my shoulder was aching very much from the constrained attitude and the pressure on the mantelpiece. I broke off, using words [talking to myself] very similar to those given by Miss G. What I muttered, as nearly as I can remember, was, 'Now, doctor, I'll get my pipe.' . . . Until within the last few weeks I have not smoked a pipe for many years, and I do not think it probable that Miss G. has ever seen me use one; but it is an absolute certainty that she was not aware I had taken to smoke one recently."

There are certain obscurities in this statement; for instance, it seems that, although Mr. Kirk speaks of the time with Miss G. being up, he was intent on trying another experiment with her. This experiment seems to have been with a diagram, but it is not clear whether it was being tried while Mr. Kirk was leaning against the mantelpiece, or subsequently, or not at all. It is likewise not obvious why Mr. Kirk thought of himself and the room, unless that was part of an experiment; but from the fact that he did not record it until after reading Miss G.'s record, we are bound to suppose that he did not regard it as such. However this may be, the coincidence between the position and actions of Mr. Kirk and the vision which Miss G. records is sufficiently striking to excuse a good deal of obscurity.

In the experiment just quoted, the scene visualized by Miss G. was the scene which was actually in Mr. Kirk's mind at the time. But in its inclusion of an hallucinatory figure of the agent himself, the experience stands nearly on the borderline between the experimental thought transference, which is the subject of the present volume, and the spontaneous telepathy, the main evidence for which is based on records of apparitions at or near the moment of death, which will form the subject of a separate volume.

The other experiment of Mr. Kirk's which will be quoted also stands near the spontaneous class, in that the object of which Miss G. became aware,

though consciously in Mr. Kirk's mind, was not
what he was trying to transfer; in fact, he was
actually trying to banish the thought of it from
his mind, thinking that it would interfere with the
success of the experiment. In this case the impression which Mr. Kirk seems to have transmitted was
recorded by him before reading Miss G.'s record,
so that this report is, in that respect, more satisfactory. On the other hand, there is less detail
in this experiment, and it is consequently less
evidential.

Mr. Kirk's report, after describing an attempt to
transfer an image of the room (this was evidently
suggested by the success of the previous week, and
a success would therefore have been discounted by
the possibility of " mental convergence ") and of
an imaginary witch, runs as follows: " Continued
to influence her some minutes after limit of time for
experiment (11.30 p.m.). During this time I was
much bothered by a subcurrent of thought, which I
in vain tried to cast off. In the morning, just
before time to get up, I had a vivid dream of my
lost dog, Laddie (lost, it appears, six years previously, but still the subject of dreams and occasional
conversation). I dreamt that the dog had returned,
and that my wife, Miss G. and myself made much of
him. I thought of him all day, and tried to suppress
the thought, fearing it would interfere with the

success of the experiments; feel worried and irritated at this, being really anxious to make an impression. Do not expect favourable result. Written same night.   J. K."

Miss G.'s report was as follows :—

" Experiment last night (9.5.92) most unsatisfactory.   Saw only a glow of light, and once for a few minutes a figure (of a vase).   Some minutes after 11.30 (the time for conclusion of experiment) it seemed as if the door of my room were open, and on the landing I saw a very large dog, moving as though it had just come upstairs.   I cannot conceive what suggested this, nor can I understand why I thought of Laddie during time of experiment.   I do not think we have mentioned him recently.   L. G."

It does not appear why Miss G. regarded this experiment as specially unsatisfactory.   If a vase had been the object selected, there would have been no reason for dissatisfaction, and similarly if Laddie had formed the subject of the designed trial, there would have been no reason for feeling surprise at his appearance or recurrence to the mind during the experiment; it is clear that Miss G. had no assurance that a vase and Laddie were *not* the subjects selected.   Consequently, her dissatisfaction and surprise are not easily accounted for.   Although the success was rather spontaneous than experimental, it was attained during the course of an arranged experiment, and falls therefore as much under the one head as the other, though such a success could not, it need hardly be said, be included in a tabular statement of the proportion of successes to failures.

Although from an evidential point of view somewhat unsatisfactory, the agent having been illiterate and apparently unable to record her experiments independently, some experiences of Dr. Gibotteau's are perhaps worth recalling here, not only as being interesting in themselves, but because of the close connexion of some of the alleged powers of the agent with the feats attributed all the world over to warlocks and wizards. Her mother had a reputation for sorcery, and Bertha herself claimed to be able, by the exercise of her will, to make people at a distance from her stumble, lose their way, or turn aside from a given path. We are not immediately concerned with these matters here; they will perhaps form the subject of another volume of the series. Three of the most striking of the experiments [1] recorded by Dr. Gibotteau resulted in one case in a visual impression alone, in one case in a visual and emotional impression, and in one case in an emotional impression alone. One night he woke up, an almost unique experience for him, at 3 in the morning. He at once thought to

[1] *Ann. des Sciences Psychiques,* vol. ii.

himself that he was the subject of an experiment, and on opening his eyes he saw opposite him on the wall a luminous patch, and a bright object as large as a melon in the middle. The following morning, it appeared, on questioning Bertha, who came to the hospital where Dr. Gibotteau was engaged, that she had made three attempts to influence him, the third being to make him see a lantern. His impression corresponded very exactly to the selected object.

On another occasion she resolved to frighten him, and chose a skeleton, of all things in the world, as an object likely to have this effect on a hospital doctor. Although he did not see or think of a skeleton, which would probably have failed in its intended effect, he had, on arriving home about midnight, a most uneasy feeling; and, although he was quite aware that it was what he called " one of Bertha's tricks," the valiant M. Gibotteau ran up to bed and put his head under the bed clothes in the briefest space possible. On another occasion Dr. Gibotteau and a friend left Bertha near her home and drove back to the Quartier Latin in a carriage which seems to have taken a somewhat devious route. On the way Dr. Gibotteau again felt an unreasoning terror, and on getting out of the carriage at the corner of the " Boul. Mich " his friend reported that he had an hallucination of something white floating before him. The following day Bertha was able, according to the report, to state that the driver had lost his way, that Dr. Gibotteau had felt afraid of nothing at all, without reason, and that they had seen some white pigeons floating round them.

The successes of Mr. Kirk and Bertha differ markedly, it should be observed, from those hitherto dealt with. In the Sidgwick experiments, it is true, pictures were externalized and seen projected on a card. But in the cases now under consideration we are dealing with full fledged hallucinations. Cases of this sort are sufficiently rare, and it is a matter for regret that more experiments in this direction do not seem to have been tried.

We have seen that Mr. Kirk, on one occasion, is recorded to have formed part of a vision. The hallucinatory dog, on the other hand, appeared to move among the objects in the vicinity of the percipient, and in this respect resembled the hallucinations commonly termed ghosts.

The recorded phenomena are, it may be noted, connected with the so-called materializations of the spiritualists, so far as they are not, as is unfortunately frequently the case, of more mundane origin, or, in other words, merely the medium dressed up to act the part. In this connexion it may be of interest to quote an early account by a good witness, or rather recorder, of an apparent case of materialization. Some two hundred and twenty years ago Sir John Reresby was governor of York. An old woman had been arraigned at the assizes as a witch, and was confined in Clifford Tower, York Castle. One of the soldiers who was on guard went to the porch to see what was causing a disturbance, and saw by the light of the moon a scroll of paper creep from under the door. This scroll then, he assured Sir John, transformed itself into a monkey, and finally turned into the shape of a turkey-cock, which passed to and fro before him. Surprised at this, as well he might be, he went to the under-keeper, and called him. The under-keeper, according to the narrative, saw neither turkey-cock nor monkey, but only the scroll of paper dancing up and down. Both witnesses seem then to have seen the scroll creep under the door again, though the space between the door and the ground was no greater than the thickness of half a crown.[1]

If this account can be depended on, it presents many curious features. Not only was the sentinel the subject of an auditory as well as of a visual hallucination, but the visual hallucination underwent an interesting series of changes, and finally reverted to its pristine form, for all the world like

[1] Reresby, *Memoirs* (London, 1734), p. 237.

the poodle in *Faust*. The hallucination was shared by a second witness, who had, we may suppose, received an account of the apparition from his comrade, and was consequently prepared to see a turkey-cock, and this witness, instead of accepting the suggestion of his fellow, saw the hallucination in its original form. So far as can be seen, the sentry also saw no more of the monkey and turkey-cock, but shared the hallucination of the dancing paper. Finally, both saw it disappear in the way it had come.

The imagination will play many tricks, and it is conceivable that the second and third forms of the sentry's hallucination were due solely to his imagination. This seems, however, an unnecessary refinement of theory, for he clearly had an hallucination of some sort, unless we suppose that both he and the under-keeper were the victims of an exceedingly ingenious trick, the mechanism for which would hardly be within the reach of a prisoner, and an old woman to boot. Unfortunately, Sir John Reresby was guiltless of a knowledge of psychical research or telepathy, or any other idea than that the story must either be a lie or literally true. Accordingly, he did not interrogate the witch, and thus perhaps missed the opportunity of handing his name down to posterity and the S.P.R. as the first man to record in due form a telepathic experience.

H

Few such experiences seem to have been recorded, though they were perhaps not uncommon in the ages when belief in witchcraft was universal, as may be seen by a reference to the *Discourse of Witchcraft*, by Fairfax, and other early detailed records of cases of alleged witchcraft. Probably one of the first instances in which experiments in this direction were tried was a case recorded by H. N. Wesermann,[1] himself the agent in the case in question and four other trials, some eighty years ago. Wesermann was a government official at Düsseldorf, and seems to have been a careful investigator. Unfortunately, he does not record how many failures there were in proportion to the five successes which he mentions. One of the trials was singularly successful, and, though the record is not exactly in the form in which the psychical researcher of the present day would put it, the case is well worth quoting.

A lady who had been dead five years was to appear to Lieutenant A. B. in a dream at 10.30 p.m., and incite him to good deeds. At half past ten, contrary to expectation, Herr A. B. had not gone to bed, but was sitting in the ante-room with a friend, Lieutenant S——, discussing the French campaign. Suddenly the door opened and a lady entered, dressed in white with a black kerchief and uncovered head; she waved her hand three times to S——

[1] *Der Magnetismus und die allgemeine Weltsprache*, p. 27.

in a friendly manner, then turned to A. B. and nodded to him, and went out again by the door.

On receiving this account from Lieutenant A. B. Wesermann was much struck by it, and wrote to the other percipient, Lieutenant S——, who lived some six miles away, for his account of it, which was as follows :—

" On the 13th of March, 1817, Herr A. B. came to pay me a visit at my lodgings, about a league from A——. He stayed the night with me, and after supper, when we both were undressed, I was sitting on the bed and Herr A. B. was standing by the door of the next room, also on the point of going to bed. This was about half-past ten. We were speaking partly about indifferent topics and partly about the events of the French campaign. Suddenly the door out of the kitchen opened without a sound and a lady entered, very pale, taller than Herr A. B., about 5 ft. 4 in. in height, strong and robust in figure, dressed in white but with a large black kerchief, which reached to below the waist. She entered with bare head, saluted me in complimentary fashion three times with her hand, turned to the left to Herr A. B. and waved her hand to him three times. After this the figure went noiselessly out without any creaking of the door. We followed at once to see if there was any deception, but found nothing."

This remarkably interesting narrative is of course from the evidential point of view very defective. We do not learn what the arrangements between Wesermann and A. B. were, whether it was merely agreed that an experiment was to be tried or whether more definite arrangements were made. We must, of course, not forget that the element of suggestion would not be one with which they would reckon as a disturbing factor. Again, it is not clear whether A. B. knew the deceased lady, nor whether, if he did, he recognized her. Nor do we know whether Herr S—— was aware of the proposed experiment.

In spite of this, the narrative is a striking one, and if a few people could be found at the present day with similar powers, it would be possible to make more rapid progress in psychical investigation. The important point of the story is that the hallucination was shared by a second percipient, who was, we may perhaps assume, ignorant of the intended trial. Even if that were not so, his narrative seems to make it clear that he was unacquainted with the deceased lady. If therefore the apparition which he saw exactly resembled her—and Wesermann assures us that it did—it is immaterial whether Wesermann and A. B. had discussed the matter previously and referred to the lady in connexion with the experiment, or not. If the narratives are accurate, and the discrepancies are insignificant, the argument for telepathy can be based on the evidence of Wesermann and Lieutenant S—— alone.

In recent years a small number of trials of a similar nature have been recorded. Some of these were published in *Phantasms of the Living*,[1] and, apart from an unfortunate defect in the record, one of these, tried by Mr. S. H. B., seems particularly good.[2] In 1884 he wrote to Mr. Gurney, telling him that he was going to try an experiment on March 22, and that he would try to make himself appear at midnight to Miss King, at 44, Norland Square, W., he himself being in a different part of London. From a subsequent statement it appears that he intended to try to touch the hair of the percipient, and if this detail had been mentioned in the preliminary letter, the evidence would have been as good as it could possibly be. With a regrettable lack of foresight, the character of the attempt was, however, not stated, and the independent evidence is thus *post facto* only, and given by Mr. Gurney, to whom Mr. B. stated shortly after the trial that this was one of the points which made the experiment successful in every detail.

The percipient signed a statement, which her sister corroborated, saying that the details were communicated to her before hearing from Mr. B.,

---

[1] *Phantasms,* i. 103 *sq.*   [2] *Loc. cit.* p. 108.

to the effect that on March 22, at about midnight, she had an impression that Mr. B. was present in her room, and came towards her and stroked her hair. The agent was informed of the success of the experiment some days after the experiment, and took down the percipient's account, which she volunteered without prompting from him, from dictation. Experiments of this sort, evidenced by contemporaneous records, are unfortunately rare. Too many experimenters are content, like Miss Verity, to record their impressions some time after their occurrence.

Another interesting case was that of the Rev. Clarence Godfrey. In 1886, after reading *Phantasms of the Living*, he was seized with a desire to try an experiment similar to the ones just summarized. According to his report, he never even mentioned that he proposed to try an experiment, much less that he proposed to try and appear " spiritually " at the foot of a lady's bed. In this respect his example is excellent, but it may be doubted whether it is altogether wise to try experiments of this sort without any warning. Even if propriety does not forbid to appear spiritually at the foot of the bed of a person of the opposite sex (it must be remembered that there are cases on record in which the agent seems to have been reciprocally aware of the surroundings of the percipient, and indeed it was to some extent the case in the present trial), care should at least be taken to discover whether an apparition of the sort described would have a bad effect on their nerves. It is very desirable to keep the evidential quality of the experiments at a high level, but it is hardly justifiable to endanger the health of one's friends in order to do so.

Mr. Godfrey tried the experiment after going to bed, and kept up the effort to appear for about eight minutes, so far as he could judge. He quickly tired, and was soon asleep. In a dream he seemed to meet the lady, and at once inquired if she had seen him. The reply was, " I was sitting beside you," and then Mr. Godfrey woke up. His watch showed 3.40 a.m.

On the following day Mr. Godfrey received from the percipient, whether spontaneously or in answer to questions is not stated, an account of the incident, which was subsequently reduced to writing. It is very unfortunate that so few people understand the necessity of recording such phenomena on the spot, not only in order to guard against any failure of memory and subsequent hallucinatory recollection, such as we are all familiar with when we attempt to recall a dream a few hours after its occurrence, and find ourselves recalling not the dream itself but rather our recollection of it as we remembered when we told the story, possibly with some embellishment, at the breakfast table.

The percipient, it appears, woke at about half past three with the impression that some one had entered her room. Experiencing a strange restless longing to leave the room, she got up and went down stairs to get some soda water. On the way back an apparition of Mr. Godfrey was seen on the staircase, dressed, not in the apparel which he actually had on at that moment, but in his usual clothes. He stood there for some seconds, and the percipient, according to her narrative, was satisfied with a very short look, and then went on upstairs, whereupon the figure vanished.

Two other trials were made by the same experimenters, one of which was a failure, being tried under unsuitable circumstances. The other was a success, though less striking perhaps than that in the first experiment.

Striking as the experiments recorded in this chapter are, they are not very numerous. In order to be evidential, such experiments require to be recorded with the most rigorous exactness, by preference, indeed, by an independent observer, who can keep his mind to the question of evidence and record details which the agent or percipient might in their absorption in their experiment fail to observe or record. The importance of this is seen in the first Kirk case, where none of the facts were recorded at the time, though Mr. Kirk himself evidently had the idea of some sort of experiment in his mind.

Not only must the record be exact in case of the successes; it must also not fail to record the failures. It is indeed desirable, where such experiments are being tried, for a record of the intended trial to be sent to the S.P.R. or other body that can be trusted to preserve it, and then for each party to the trial to post their reports immediately after the trial, making such additions as may seem necessary at a later date. The faculty is probably a rare one, and perhaps not one per cent. of the total number of trials would show any result. Given, however, an agent and percipient who do achieve some measure of success, and their percentage may reach seventy or eighty per cent. The case for telepathy will then, it is clear, not rest on the proportion between the total number of trials and the total number of successes, but on the proportions in the trials by the more gifted experimenters, always provided· that their series are sufficiently long to exclude chance coincidence as a probable cause.

CHAPTER VII

Telepathic Hypnotism—Telepathic Dreams

ALTHOUGH, properly speaking, the production of the hypnotic state by means of mental suggestion does not fall within the limits of a work dealing with thought transference, inasmuch as it cannot be alleged that any idea is, or appears to be, transferred, the subject of the induction of sleep, either at a distance or from close quarters without verbal or other means which influence the patient through the ordinary channels of sense, is sufficiently germane to the subject under discussion to make an outline of some of the more important experiments desirable at this point.

It has already been pointed out that some of the magnetizers detected, or believed that they detected, what they termed community of sensation between the operator and his patient. Many of these early experiments are, however, of little value evidentially, for the very simple reason that suggestion was unrecognized in the days when all the phenomena were put down to the passage of a magnetic fluid. Even in the case of experiments in our own day when this source of error is sufficiently well known, we cannot always be sure that it is sufficiently guarded against, when the operator and patient are in close proximity. Apropos of the clever horse Hans, whose performances have puzzled the scientific men, or some of them, of Germany, a story has been told of a dog belonging to Sir William Huggins. This dog, either with or without training, it was not quite clear which from the narrative, gained the power of interpreting its master's unconscious indications so greatly that it was able to select from a pile of letters the one chosen by him, even though he stood behind the dog and out of its sight, the explanation being that when the dog in trying letter after letter arrives at the right one, the subtle change in the respiratory movements of its master, or some equally recondite source of information, gives it the necessary clue. The thinking horse's performances are, of course, on a different plane. There can be no doubt that he had been deliberately trained to take cognizance of the signals of his master. The only remarkable point about the affair is that any ordinarily acute man should have been puzzled by the trick; much more a man of science from the Fatherland, some of whose sons make it their boast that " psychical research and all that humbug " may find a home in England, but never for a moment imposes on

the more acute Teutonic man of science. About
this, however, it is possible to hold another opinion.[1]

If a mere dog can thus seize the clues unconsciously given and deal with matters which it does
not in the least comprehend, like letters and numbers, it is clear that human beings may far more
readily pick up slight indications, the interpretation of which will enable them to carry out the will
of the operator in matters of which they are fully
cognizant. While, therefore, it by no means follows
that all experiments carried out when the agent
and patient are within earshot of each other are
necessarily subject to this criticism, it is clear that
their evidential quality must be inferior to others,
equally good in results, carried out when agent and
patient are so far removed as to make appreciation
of the wishes of the agent a greater miracle if it is
due to the operation of the ordinary senses than it
would be if it were due to that other means of
communication to which the name of telepathy is
given.

Fortunately, there is more than one well-attested
case of the induction of hypnotic sleep under due
precautions by operators of reputation in the world

[1] Since the above was written a committee has reported
that there is no evidence of anything beyond quick apprehen-
sion of his master's signs on the part of the horse. The two
committees seem to have been independent.

of science, when the distance between agent and patient was such as to make the hypothesis of ordinary sense transmission absolutely absurd. The first of these is the case of Madame B., a French peasant woman, on whom Dr. Gibert of Havre and Dr. Pierre Janet tried experiments in 1885 and 1886, some of them in the presence of members of the Society for Psychical Research.

Before describing the experiments in question, it may be well to say that the patient had shown herself remarkably susceptible, and that there were indications that the hypnotic state was produced rather by the operator's will than by any of his acts, even when he was in her presence and actually in contact with her. Dr. Janet remarks, for example, that it was necessary, in order to entrance Madame B., to concentrate one's thought intensely on the suggestion to sleep which was given her; the more the operator's thought wandered, the more difficult it was to induce the trance. This influence of the operator's thought, however extraordinary it may seem, predominates in this case to such an extent that it replaces all other causes. If one presses Madame B.'s hand without the thought of hypnotizing her, the trance is not induced; but, on the other hand, it is possible to send her to sleep by thinking of it without pressing her hand.

For the reasons mentioned above, this class of experiment is hardly conclusive, and can never be made conclusive, however careful the experimenters may be. *A fortiori* is it impossible to record the experiments in such a way as to make it clear to the reader that the precautions taken were sufficient. When we essay experiments at a distance, however, the case is otherwise. Not only are the necessary precautions far simpler, but there is never any necessity for hurry. The observers can record at their leisure, and the attention to detail thus rendered possible should put an ordinarily intelligent reporter in a position to make clear to his readers exactly what happened. It is impossible here to give the experiments in detail. Those who desire to judge of the precautions taken, and of the completeness of the record, must refer to Prof. Janet's paper on the subject in the *Revue Phil.* (Aug., 1886), or to the account in the *Proc. S.P.R.* (iv. 127, sq.).

It may be mentioned that the distance between the operator and the subject was in no case less than a quarter of a mile, sufficient, one may imagine, to exclude the operation of suggestion through the ordinary senses. One determined opponent of telepathy, however, has been found to suggest, either in this or in a similar case, that the subject became aware of an attempt to hypnotize her, because the mental concentration on the part of the operator increased the arterial tension in his circulatory system, and that though the distance between operator and subject was at the least several hundred yards, such was the state of hyperæsthesia to which the latter, for no reason assignable, had been brought, that she was able at that distance to hear the change in the throb of the agent's arteries, and from the change to infer that he was trying to hypnotize her. Of a truth science has her miracles, especially when some obnoxious fact has to be explained in some respectable manner. Not the least miracle is that any sane man should be found to suggest that such a state of hyperæsthesia may exist and yet not be detected by trained physiologists who are conducting the experiments. The state of mind of such a critic is only comparable to that of the insurance company's expert who assured the court, in a disputed case, that slipping on a piece of banana skin was evidence of a dangerous mental state, and that the policy of an assured person who made a claim for an accident of a different kind should be held to be invalid, because he had concealed from the company, at the time of effecting his insurance, that he had once sprained his knee through slipping on a piece of banana skin.

As a disproof of the hypothesis of accidental

coincidence, it may be mentioned that Madame B. only twice, so far as is known, fell into a hypnotic trance spontaneously during several weeks that she was under observation; not only so, but on one of these occasions it was clear that it was only a relapse into a hypnotic trance from which she had been insufficiently awakened; in the other case she entranced herself by looking at the picture of her hypnotist, Dr. Gibert, which is very far indeed from being a case of ordinary spontaneous trance, especially if, as is possible, Dr. Gibert had ever entranced her by the method of staring at her.

In all, from October, 1885, to May in the following year, twenty-five experiments were tried. Of these nineteen only were reckoned as successes, though in several other cases there was a more or less marked influence on the patient. As a typical case may be quoted the experiment of April 24, 1886, as described by F. W. H. Myers: "On April 24, the whole party [consisting of F. W. H. Myers, A. T. Myers, Dr. Gibert, Prof. Janet, Dr. Ochorowicz, and my late friend, Léon Marillier] chanced to meet at M. Janet's house at 3 p.m., and he then at my (i.e. F. W. H. Myers's) suggestion entered his study to will that Madame B. should sleep. We waited in his garden, and at 3.20 proceeded together to the Pavilion (where Madame B. resided with a sister of Dr. Gibert's), which I entered first at 3.30, and found Madame B. profoundly sleeping over her sewing, having ceased to sew. Becoming talkative, she said to M. Janet " C'est vous qui m'avez commandé." She said she fell asleep at 3.5 p.m.

From this narrative it is clear that the selection of the time was in the hands of an entirely independent person. It would, of course, be ridiculous to suppose that Prof. Janet was in collusion with Madame B., but experience of the foolish objections urged against apparently perfect experiments teaches one to meet every possible and impossible criticism. The party having met by chance, there was no possibility of M. Janet's having accidentally communicated to Madame B.; that they were likely to meet at the hour of 3 p.m.; consequently auto-suggestion on her part seems to be excluded. Bearing in mind the remarkable appreciation of time by hypnotized subjects, to which the experiments of Dr. Milne Bramwell bear such conclusive testimony, we may fairly conclude that the hour given by Madame B. as that at which she was entranced was nearly correct. The only criticism possible, and that affects only a very minor item of the case, is that Madame B. may have gone to sleep earlier or later instead of at almost exactly the time at which Prof. Janet willed her to go to sleep, and that her mention of the hour of 3.5 was due to a suggestion somehow conveyed unintentionally by one of the party—a thing improbable in itself, and almost certain to have attracted the attention of one or other of the trained observers who made up the party. It might indeed also be objected that Madame B. was only simulating sleep; but against this hypothesis must be put the testimony of men of great experience in such matters that she was really entranced. It might also be objected in the particular case under discussion that she may have observed the approach of the party, and that this operated as a suggestion. But in reply to this it suffices to point out that she named as the hour when she entered the trance a period before the party had come in sight of the Pavilion, or even left the garden of M. Janet's house; and secondly, that she was in some of the experiments kept under observation by some of the party, so far as possible without disclosing their presence to her for fear of the knowledge that she was being observed operating as a suggestion or otherwise interfering with the success of the experiments, and that the suggestions of the distant operator were carried out under circumstances which preclude the possibility of their having been in some way transmitted by one of the observers through the ordinary channels of the subject's senses.

This successful series of experiments was followed by another in the autumn of the same year, in which the measure of success was far less, though still considerably above what could be attributed to chance coincidence. A summary of the results will be found in the *Proc. S.P.R.*, v. 43-45. Though the diminished number of successes, to some extent, lessens the evidential value of the whole series, it should not be overlooked that, if telepathy is a fact, such variation is exactly what might be expected. Both portions of the whole series being above expectation, it cannot be contended that later failures cause the argument founded on the earlier results to fall to the ground.

The argument for mental suggestion from the facts of hypnotism apparently at a distance gains much force from a series of extraordinarily careful experiments on the same subject, tried by Prof. Richet in Paris with the same subject, whom he designates by the name of Léonie. These trials are discussed by M. Richet with great acuteness and absence of bias in *Proc. S.P.R.*, v. 18 *sq.*, and although he only claims that two of his nine trials were successful, and four partially successful, his canons of evidence are so high that this proportion is sufficiently striking. Prof. Richet's narrative is an exact *résumé* of his notes made each day immediately after such experiment, and cannot be abridged without diminishing its value as evidence; I therefore refrain from reproducing them here, and merely refer my readers to M. Richet's own words—

" It is important to notice that in all these experiments the trance not infrequently supervened some time after the operator willed it; on the other hand, there is not a single clear case where the patient was entranced too soon, and on the few doubtful cases no stress can be laid. In considering the possibility of coincidence and auto-suggestion this feature is of much importance."

In a work dealing with telepathy the subject of dreams cannot be entirely neglected, though evidence drawn from them is, in more than one respect, less satisfactory than that drawn from experiences in the normal waking state or the hypnotic sleep. In the first place, dreams are extraordinarily numerous and varied. There is therefore a great danger of improper selection. Even where any one sets him or herself to experiment systematically there is always the possibility that they have had several dreams on one night, or, it may be, a multitude of dreams on one night, for there is no way of finding out how much we dream except by recalling them in our waking hours, and we have no assurance that the dreams recalled when we wake are more than a small proportion of the whole number which an automatic record, if such a thing were possible, would have shown to have passed through our minds, or that part of them which is occupied in producing dreams. Now the evidence for telepathy is not likely, in the long run, to be over-estimated, so far as it is based on results with dreams, for we can readily secure that there shall be no undue selection in the way of recording only those dreams which show a connexion with the selected subject. All that is necessary is for the dreamer to record before hearing from the agent all available data with regard to the dreams, and for no subsequent modification of the recollection of the dreams to be allowed any weight.

But, on the other hand, the evidence for telepathy may easily be under-estimated. If A is in the habit of dreaming ten times each night, we may assume that an attempt at mental suggestion will only influence a certain proportion of these at most, possibly only one. Now, if A has a telepathic dream every night, but habitually forgets nine out of his ten dreams, he will recall his successful telepathic dream only once in ten nights; the result of this will be that the experiments will show only one-tenth of the proportion of successes which were, as a matter of fact, attained. The difficulty may indeed be, to some extent, overcome by a suggestion from the agent that the dream to be remembered is the dream telepathically induced; and if telepathy is a fact this should operate to diminish the cause of failure, or apparent failure, just alluded to. Even then, however, we cannot be sure that the statistics are not erroneous. Experiments in which the subject cannot recall his experiences with accuracy, nor yet describe them at the moment of their occurrence, can only occupy a subordinate place in the psychical scheme.

Not only is it difficult to make sure that all dreams are recalled, but it is even more difficult to recall the details even of those dreams which we know to have occurred. At the moment of waking perhaps they are, or seem to be, fresh in our memories, but almost before we have got pencil and paper to note them down they are gone. Sometimes they are revived again in the evening. We all (or if not all, at any rate many of us) know that an inebriated subject will sometimes, like a somnambulist, take an object and put it away; in his sober moments he quite fails to recall the fact, or if he recalls it, he forgets the locality in which the object is deposited. It is possible, however, to reawaken his memory of the incident by reducing him again to a state of inebriation. The same thing perhaps occurs, though to a less noticeable extent, in our transition from wakefulness to sleep, and *vice versâ*. The facts of the dream, remembered in the morning before we are fully awake, are recalled at night when we reach the same stage of sleepiness. But this naturally does not help us to record the dream; the cause which prevented us from doing so in the morning is there in the evening, and there is the additional difficulty that we are probably resigned to getting up in the morning, whereas in the evening we are very far from being anxious to rouse ourselves.

Here too, perhaps, suggestion might be useful. So far as I know, no experiments of any importance in this direction have been tried, but it would be interesting to see how far suggestion succeeds in recalling to the ordinary person the dreams which have passed through his mind a few hours previously, only to be forgotten as soon as the full stream of waking consciousness begins to flow.

Many coincidental dreams have, of course, been recorded. With them, however, we are not concerned. We have only to deal with the cases in which the dream was or appeared to be the outcome of a pre-arranged experiment. Allusion has already been made to the striking experiment recorded by Wesermann, and it will be recollected that the experiment was to have resulted in a dream of the lady whose apparition was seen by the two officers. The four other cases recorded by Wesermann are also of the same class, and in their case nothing interfered with carrying out the trial as originally arranged. We have, however as remarked above, no certainty that Wesermann recorded his failurès as well as his successes, and this virtually invalidates his narratives from the point of view of evidence, so far as the dream cases are concerned; the apparition is, of course, in a different class, for it was probably the only case of its kind.

A long and interesting series of experiments tried by Dr. Ermacora, of Padua, with a child between three and four years old, are of some interest.[1] He was experimenting in 1892 with a medium for automatic writing and other phenomena. Accident suggested that a little girl, a cousin of the medium's, of the age of three and a half, was a good telepathic subject, and Dr. Ermacora undertook a long series of trials, the object of which was to see how far a personality that manifested itself by automatic writing was able to induce telepathic dreams in the child. So far as Dr. Ermacora is concerned there is no reason to suppose that any precautions which he considered desirable to avoid verbal or other ordinary forms of suggestion were omitted. But he seems to have assumed the good faith of the medium and her relatives, and this in view of some experience in the matter seems to me to be un-

[1] *Proc. S.P.R.* v. 255-308.

desirable. Not only professional mediums but amateurs who have nothing to gain in a pecuniary sense from success or failure are quite capable of attempting, and do actually attempt, to deceive investigators in a way that would be astonishing if it were less common.

Although but few records of the experiments have been published, the telepathic trials between Dr. van Eeden and Mrs. Thompson cannot be passed over. Mrs. Thompson is a Hampstead lady, not a professional medium, whose trance phenomena are of great interest. Among other members of the S.P.R. who have had sittings with her is Dr. van Eeden, of Bussum, Holland. At the close of a series of sittings at the end of 1899 it was arranged that Nelly, a personality that appears, together with others, in Mrs. Thompson's trance, should make an attempt to enter into communication with Dr. van Eeden after his return to Holland. It should be mentioned that Dr. van Eeden has been in the habit of observing his dreams for a long time, and that he can carry out in his dreams actions which he has planned to execute. In pursuance of this scheme he made up his mind to call Nelly on the first occasion on which he had, what he terms, "a clear dream," that is, one in which his volition is sufficiently active to permit him to execute what he has previously planned.

The last sitting at which Dr. van Eeden was present in 1899 was held on December 4. On January 3 Dr. van Eeden recorded in his diary that on the previous night he had had a clear dream, and called Nelly. His account goes on: " She appeared to me in the form of a little girl, rather plump and healthy-looking, with loose, light-coloured hair. . . . This was the second dream of the sort after my stay in England. The first occurred on December 11. In this dream I also tried to call Nelly, but it was no success."

The first point to be noted in connexion with this incident is that between December 4 and the night of January 2-3 five sittings at least had been held with Mrs. Thompson, and at none of them did Nelly make any remark about any summons from Dr. van Eeden. On January 5, however, she remarked, " Tell Dr. van Eeden he kept calling me last night." It is true there is a mistake of a day here, but it is easy to make too much of an error of this sort. For it should not be forgotten that Nelly is inaccurate with regard to dates, even when they relate to incidents of which she shows supernormal knowledge. (It is impossible to deal with this question here, however, at length. It must be postponed to a future volume on trance-mediumship.)

The next point is that Dr. van Eeden describes

Nelly as having light hair. Now at a sitting on November 29, at which Dr. van Eeden was present, Nelly had described herself as having black curly hair. The dream figure was therefore by no means what we should expect if Dr. van Eeden's mind alone had been operative in producing it.

At a later sitting Nelly, it is true, described herself as having light hair (this was on January 18, so that it had nothing to do with Dr. van Eeden's idea of Nelly). On a subsequent occasion Nelly, however, stated that the description of January 18 referred not to herself but to Elsie, another personality who appears in Mrs. Thompson's trances. (On this question see the reports of the sittings, *Proc. S.P.R.,* xvii. 113.) Whether this is so or not, the interesting point is that, on January 18, Nelly stated that Elsie had been to Dr. van Eeden in December, and that her description of Elsie, which was absolutely independent, so far as normally acquired knowledge goes, of Dr. van Eeden's account of his dream visitor, tallies with the latter, although Dr. van Eeden was expecting to see quite a different person.

In the third place, Nelly stated on January 5 that Dr. van Eeden was in bed, alone, not with his wife, and that he was " inside those curtains." Dr. van Eeden writes that these particulars are correct; he was alone, and curtains, or rather drapery, was before the bed. Slight therefore though the incident is, there are no material errors of detail, the only one being the post-dating of the dream, which is unimportant, whereas antedating would, of course, have been a fatal flaw.

Dr. van Eeden's next clear dream was on January 15. At the sitting with Mrs. Thompson on the following day Nelly made no allusion to it, but on January 18 she stated that Elsie had told her before January 16 that " Old Whiskers " in the bed was calling her. Nelly's reply was " Bother Whiskers! You go," and she added " and very likely she did go."

In view of the fact that Nelly says she was told by another trance personality, it is of considerable interest that Dr. van Eeden accidentally, as he noted in his diary, began to call Elsie in his dream instead of Nelly. It is also worthy of note that this dream visitor appeared. This agrees with Nelly's statement that she did not go.

Trivial as the incidents may appear, they are evidentially important when we reflect how remote is the probability that Nelly would hit upon the dates and details by accident, and that Dr. van Eeden, on his side, would see a figure corresponding to Nelly's description, though not to his own expectation, on the one occasion out of three clear dreams when Nelly stated that a visit had been paid to him. As bearing on the possibility of co-incidence, it may be mentioned that after Dr. van Eeden had left England, and before the sitting at which his name was first mentioned, five, and before the next dream two, seances had been held. In other words, it was ten to one against the right dates being hit upon by chance.

Unfortunately, the evidential value of the dream cases is diminished by subsequent ill-success. Though it can hardly be said that definite wrong statements were made, and Nelly showed on two occasions knowledge of Dr. van Eeden's state of health, she did not succeed in giving any evidential details with regard to dream conversations, and this must, to some extent, diminish the value of the cases quoted above.

Whatever be our conclusion with regard to the part played by the trance personalities in the production of the dreams, it cannot be denied that the experiments are interesting. How far the average man is likely to be able to control his dreams, as Dr. van Eeden does, it is difficult to say. My own dreams are too few in number for me to make any progress in that direction, and perhaps in most cases the necessary patience will be found to be lacking. Probably most people would hardly be content to observe their dreams, and experiment for a long period with little or no result. F. W. H.

Myers has recorded that thrice only in the course of some 10,000 dreams was he able to control their course, and his interest in psychical investigation and patience in collecting material is shared by few. Even if some of my readers find themselves in a position to influence their sleeping thoughts, they will perhaps be at a loss how to experiment, for lack of a reliable medium with a trance personality prepared to experiment. Although it might be worth while, in default of anything better, to utilize the services of an ordinary mortal whose life is uncomplicated by trances, a better plan will be to communicate with the *S.P.R.*, who have more opportunity of finding a co-experimenter of the right brand, and will doubtless welcome the opportunity of adding to their list of sane people with psychical interests and accomplishments.

CHAPTER VIII

EXPERIMENTS IN 1902

Pictures—Colours—Diagrams

I NOW turn to the experiments carried on in the rooms of the S.P.R., and mainly directed by myself. Up to the end of March 1902, they were conducted at 19, Buckingham Street, in the small room. The percipient and agent were about seven feet apart, facing in the same direction and separated by a double screen with cloth on one side and wall (?) paper on the other. There were two cupboards with glass doors, one on each side of the fireplace. The agent and percipient were so placed that neither could see the other reflected in either of these doors. With the exception of a picture over the fireplace, equally incapable of disclosing to the percipient the movements of the agent or the object he was contemplating, there was no other reflecting surface in the room to act as a disturbing element.

The screen was close to my writing table, in such a position that I could watch both agent and percipient at the same time and hand to the former, without the knowledge of the latter, the object, card, or diagram to be mentally transferred. In the record everything is noted which was said by the agent or any one acquainted with the object; other remarks, by myself for example, when I was only recording without a knowledge of what the agent was thinking of or looking at, are only noted when they bear on the experiment in the way of suggesting a remark by the percipient.

The objects were in every case kept in closed boxes until the experiments began; they were then withdrawn from the box in such a position that they could not be seen by the percipient and were at once handed to the agent. At the close of the experiment (or of a series) the success or otherwise was announced, and the objects replaced in the boxes, and in the case of diagrams, colours, numbers or cards, thoroughly shuffled. In the case of the diagrams they were, when not specially noted, prepared by myself before the experiments began; but in order to simplify the calculation of probabilities it may be assumed that the percipients were acquainted with them.

The word " chosen " indicates that the object was intentionally selected, the word " drawn " that it was selected by lot or at random.

The agent and percipient were, in all cases subsequently dealt with, members or associates of the S.P.R. and, as a rule, already known to me personally. In several cases agent and percipient met for the first time at the experiments in which they took part.

PICTURES.

The first experiment of those to be mentioned here, was tried on January 27, 1902; present—Miss T. (percipient), Messrs. W. W. Baggally (agent), J. G. Piddington and N. W. Thomas (recorder). Mr. Piddington arrived first, bringing with him, as I subsequently learnt, a copy of the *Windsor Magazine,* which he placed in a closed box behind the screen. The recorder did not, except when specially noted, see any object before the end of the experiment, and notes as to the object were, in each case, not made until after the experiment was over.

The percipient took her seat with her back to the light in a low wicker chair, and was asked to look in a crystal ball. After seeing a figure she described a luminous appearance and went on, " Now I see a sort of cloudy thing that might be a landscape, very indistinct. I can see a curious light in the centre; is that a reflection? [J.G.P.] Does it come through your landscape? [Miss T.] Yes. There is a river and mountains, and a group of trees on the left. [N. W. T.] Your left? [Miss T.] Yes. [J. G. P.] Is one part more prominent? [Miss T.] No, it might be Alps or Lucerne where I have just been."

K ·

The scene had disappeared when Miss T. looked again, but immediately after she went on, " Now it has come back to the landscape, snow peaks, the river clearer, rushing down, a group of cottages or houses towards the background on the left. [J. G. P.] Anything on the bank? [Miss T.] I was thinking I saw some boats on the bank, the one nearer me; it might be a lot of wood. [J. G. P.] Are you close to it? [Miss T.] There is a lot of foliage or something of that sort in the immediate foreground; the river *is* in the foreground, but further back. Those people—it's very queer—it's an exact copy of my brain; I've seen the scene."

Up to this point, Miss T. was not aware that any thought transference was being attempted. Between the two descriptions reported above, J. G. P. showed N. W. T. the cover of current number of the *Windsor Magazine*, holding it a few inches beyond the screen and putting it flat on the writing-table, where it remained for about five seconds. It was impossible for Miss T. to have seen it either directly or by reflection. Her eyes, too, were, as J. G. P. afterwards informed me, as a rule, closed. J. G. P. was, when he showed me the cover, on the same side of the screen as the agent, and was invisible from where Miss T. sat. The word Windsor was not mentioned nor any reference made to the object.

As a matter of fact Mr. Piddington had, before

[PLATE II.

WINDSOR CASTLE.

To face p. 131.

the point at which the notes above quoted begins, handed Mr. Baggally the *Windsor Magazine*; unknown to the recorder, Mr. Baggally, who was behind the screen, had been steadily gazing at the picture on the cover, here reproduced for comparison (Pl. II). It will hardly be denied that the resemblance was striking; but this was not all.

At 3.47, seventeen minutes after the experiment began, Miss T. took pencil and paper to try automatic writing. The trials were made without success, and one colour trial. At about 4 o'clock a diagram was tried, but the drawing was again without resemblance to the object. Later Miss T. closed her eyes to try to get visual impressions, and then remarked that she saw a lot of pictures, mentioning three—a field of wheat, a garden, and Windsor Castle, the latter being especially clear, with the river below.

Two other experiments were then tried and resulted in failures.

A comparison of the description with the illustration shows how close the resemblance was. It is, of course, impossible to estimate the probabilities in a case of this sort, but the experiment seemed worth recording here in detail to show the sort of trial which good crystal gazers may with advantage make.

Several further series of experiments were tried

with Miss T. in April and May, 1902, with varying success. The trials took place in the rooms of the Society, at 20, Hanover Square, W.; the agent and percipient were separated by a double cloth screen, six feet high, and the objects were kept in an American roll-top desk, and in closed boxes until the percipient was seated, and in such a position as not to be able to see what object was selected.

Shorthand notes of descriptions by the percipient were taken by the Society's shorthand writer, Miss Keates, and a record of the conditions of the experiment and of the objects was kept by myself or, in my absence, by another recorder.

On April 23, eleven trials were made, four with pictures and seven with diagrams. The first picture selected was from Warne's *Easy A.B.C. Painting Book* and was the right-hand half of the coloured picture to O; this represented a long-eared owl sitting on the branch of a tree growing from a trunk on the right of it, which was covered with ivy; in the background, a mass of high-trees, and behind them the moon represented as pure white without spots and partly concealed by them so as to be only semi-circular, in such a position as to form a halo round the owl's head. Below the ivy in the foreground and between it and the margin of the page, was white uncoloured paper of a breadth of more than half an inch. One has the impression that the owl is high in the air. This picture was from a book bought some weeks previously, used for the experiment and then kept in the drawer of my secretaire until the experiment on the present occasion. It was taken from my secretaire by myself and handed to the agent, Mr. W. W. Baggally, who was already seated behind the screen. Miss Keates, who took the shorthand notes of all that was said, whether by Miss T. or any one else, and Mr. G. Musgrove, who was also present, remained in ignorance of what had been selected.

Miss T. after seating herself facing Miss Keates, but, with her back to the light, to myself and to the agent, who was behind the screen, took the crystal and said, after a few minutes : "Well, it is very indistinct, but what it seems to me is a forest, very high trees in the foreground, and then there is a group of animals in it and there is a large ———. There is a brilliant light in the centre of the picture, but I cannot make out what it is. It seems like the sun. [Rec.[1]] What shape is it? [Miss T.] The shape of the Aurora Borealis. [Rec.] And is it uniformly white or what colour? [Miss T.] It is a white dazzling light, the centre is dark. It is so brilliant, it makes my eyes tired. It is quite in the background. [Rec.] What is in the foreground, then? [Miss T.] Why, it's like the sea, like a forest, trees

[1] N. W. Thomas.

on one side and water in the front. [Rec.] Is there anything else you can see in the picture? [Miss T.] I have described everything I can see; there is a great deal more, it is very indistinct. Have you got a magnifying glass? (One brought.) Men, a group of men passing to one side of the picture. I rather think I must have seen it in South Africa. Now it is fading."

It will be seen that, with the exception of the animals at the beginning and the men at the end, the description is singularly accurate. Several points might have been further elucidated, but the percipient was in a dreamy condition and had to be questioned before she said anything. The picture faded before questions could be asked as to which side the trees were on, and what the dark mass in the centre of the light was. The following points were correctly described: the moon, with a dark object in the centre, in the background, not a complete circle but the shape of the Aurora (i.e. semicircular); the trees on one side in the foreground; possibly the white paper appears as water.

The next two pictures were: L and D, both failures. After a success with a diagram, described below, there was another unsuccessful picture, R, in the same book.

On April 25, four experiments in crystal gazing were tried by Mrs. M. with Miss P. as agent. The first object was a picture of a parrot on a bar with a seed box at each end. The only impression was that of " a sort of long stalk with a bulb on the end of it." This was correct as far as it went, but hardly entitles us to count the trial as even partially successful. The next two trials resulted in the percipient seeing diagrams instead of pictures, and the last, though some resemblance could be traced, was equally unsuccessful.

On April 29, Miss T. was again the percipient. Five trials were made with pictures. The first subject was the third coloured picture in Warne's *Merry Moments Painting Book,* representing a river or narrow lake in the centre running at the foot of some hills in the right background. In the left foreground a child fishing, just behind her some bushes, no background.

The book was purchased by myself on the day in question, and I reached the rooms simultaneously with Miss T. It was, however, put behind the screen unopened. Besides the agent, Mr. Baggally, Mr. Piddington saw the picture selected by myself. The conditions were as described before.

Miss T. said, " I get the impression of a figure; it is a figure. I cannot see whether it is a man or woman, but it is dressed in some sort of flowing drapery in the distance. It seems as if it were walking in front of a terrace; in the distance, there

is a slight suggestion of a man. It is a very ———.
There seems something walking into a room, rather
into the interior of a palace. That melts away.
There is a broad sheet of water, and there is a sky
in the distance, and it is very bright on the horizon.
That is all I see. [Rec.] Anything on the sheet of
water? [Miss T.] Well there is something that looks
vaguely like a ship, but that might be a suggestion
by the water. It looks like a ship. Have you got
a magnifying glass? I see something on the ship.
The ship seems approaching nearer, and as it ap-
proaches you can see something moving on it. I
don't know what it is. It is melting away."

The resemblance here cannot be called more than
slight. The sheet of water, however, is correct,
and the figure though displaced to the background
is fairly described.

The second, third, and fourth experiments were
failures.

Mrs. Thompson arrived during the experiment
and went into the library, where she was joined by
Mr. Piddington. It was arranged that she should
act as agent. The object, the head on an Edward
VII half-sovereign, was selected by J. G. Piddington. N. W. Thomas, controlling the whole experiment, W. W. Baggally, and Miss Keates taking
notes of what Miss T. said, remained in ignorance
of it until the experiment was over.

Miss T. said: " I can't get a clear impression, I get the impression of a figure. It is very, very vague, much more vague than the others. It is so vague I can hardly tell whether it is a figure or an animal. That is all I get. There is 'one thing in the whole picture." The picture developed into three figures subsequently, but this may be regarded as a normal occurrence with Miss T., whose crystal visions were almost invariably living pictures. There is possibly some connexion between the object and the impression, but the latter was too vague for any stress to be laid on it.

On May 6, three experiments were tried, all failures, with agent and percipient in different rooms. Two with another percipient also failed.

On May 13, four experiments were tried under the same conditions. In the first the object was a picture of an old man with a load of faggots, shaking hands with a young girl. Miss T. saw in the crystal a figure which might have been a bear on its hind legs. The second was a failure. The third was a picture of a small building with a circular tower at one end, that had a curious peaked roof like an extinguisher; on the right was another building, and the immediate foreground was white. Miss T. said, " This looks like a building on a hill, and a lake in front, whether it is a church I cannot see. It is a mass of buildings, very like a scene in Switzerland." The resemblance was not close, but it was not altogether absent.

In the fourth experiment, Miss T. saw one tall object going up to a sharp point. The object actually was Snowdon from Portmadoc, but the description was perhaps a continuation of that in the previous experiment, a postponed impression of the tower.

Several short series of experiments with pictures were tried at Buckingham Street, in February and March, with various percipients. Of four trials on February 28, the only one worthy of note was that with the picture of the owl described above (p. 132). The percipient, Miss P., saw in the crystal " a figure of some sort; rather like a woman, oldish, something on her head, a sort of cap. Like a caricature." This can perhaps hardly be regarded as a success, but, on the other hand, the owl as a caricature of an old woman is not a far-fetched idea, and the cap is supplied by the moon surrounding the head of the bird.

The same picture was used a week later with another percipient, Mrs. C., who, between two failures, described " a man's head on a pillow, about 50 or 60, with a beard." The resemblance is at best very remote, but possibly the moon suggested the pillow.

On the same day a picture series was tried, with Mrs. Verrall and Miss P. as agents. The only approximation to a success in the six trials with pictures was when Miss P. mentioned the letter B in connexion with a picture marked, unknown to her, $\dfrac{B}{41}$.

Experience shows that estimates of probabilities differ very widely in cases where exact statistical methods are not available. I therefore refrain from summing up the net results of such experiments, both here and later. It is perhaps worthy of note that some success was attained with the owl picture on each occasion it was used.

Colours

At various times a number of trials with colours were made. These experiments are much complicated by the difficulty which most percipients have in naming the colours they see. There are, as a matter of fact, at least 360 names of colours in English, probably more if names derived from flowers and other natural objects are included. In some of the experiments a numbered sheet of colours corresponding to those used by the agent was hung before the percipient; and this was found to work well in some cases. The matter is further complicated by possible influence of secondary colours and after images, though such influence was not traced in any individual case. Another source of difficulty is that the agent did not always see the colours in a bright light.   The result of this was to deaden them; on one occasion, for example, bronze was described by the percipient as sepia brown. I was preparing to mark this down a failure, but the agent said that in the dull light the bronze was almost exactly the colour named by the percipient.   Under these circumstances the trial was counted as a success.

Twenty-one trials were made on various occasions with cards of the following colours—red, blue, bronze, yellow, green, black cross. Of these trials a brightish red was described as pink by one percipient; another percipient saw pink, then something dark, and yellow (this was counted a failure); canary yellow was given as yellow; mauve, as blue, red as pink, and brown as brown; on a subsequent occasion the same percipient failed four successive times.

On May 13, Miss T. made four trials, the agents and percipient being in different rooms.   Red was again described as pink; a rainbow effect with prevailing colour violet was seen when blue would have been correct; a bright yellow dog was seen when one agent had yellow, the other bronze; the fourth trial was a failure.

If we count the red = pink as a success, and it should be noted that all the percipients agreed in getting the impression of pink when the agent was looking at this colour, with which there were no failures, other than such misdescription as is involved in calling it pink, we have 6 complete successes, and two partial successes out of 21 trials, the rainbow effect being counted a failure. The expectation was 3½.

On the same day a series of trials took place in a studio, with four percipients. The only one of these to get results above expectation was Miss P., who was also markedly successful in the diagram trials to be described later. With myself as agent she named a card of the next shade to the one required, 5 times out of 20 trials, and a card of the same colour, but more remote shade, 5 times more, the total number of colours being 20, arranged in 4 rows, and the expectation in each case, therefore, 3 and 2½. Twenty trials with other agents were, on the whole, failures.

The conditions were here quite satisfactory, as the agent was seated in a gallery, and though his voice was audible to the percipients, he was quite invisible. A sheet of colours, numbered to correspond with those used by the agent, who drew coloured cards at random, served to identify the percipient's impressions. The colours in this series were not the same as those previously described. They included several shades of red, blue, yellow, green, brown, grey, etc.

Diagrams and Numbers

As in the case of pictures, a statistical discussion
of the success or failure of trials with diagrams is,
in the nature of things, impossible.[1]   In the first
place, no exhaustive enumeration of all possible
diagrams can be made; we have not therefore any
basis on which to calculate the number from
which a selection might be taken to be made.   In
the second place, it frequently happens that the
reproduction contains a sufficient number of the
elements of the original diagram to enable us to
see a resemblance, even when the trial is not completely successful.   But *pari passu* with the intro-
duction of alien elements, or the elimination of
the original elements, arises the difficulty of determining how far, if at all, the trial has been successful, and how far the presence of a few points of resemblance is due to coincidence; for it must be
noted that the number of independent elements is
very few, and the complexity of a thought transference diagram is limited, far more than is the
case with a picture of which many details are
known and need not be specially noted by the
agent, such as for example, the lines and shading

[1] If we assume that all the diagrams were known to the
percipient, and deal only with complete successes, statistical methods are available; but this excludes much of the
evidence.

that go to suggest water in motion, by the power
of the agent to grasp it in its entirety and by the
power of the percipient to reproduce it correctly,
almost, if not entirely, from memory.

Only by facsimiles of the originals and reproductions is it possible to put the evidence forward in
such a manner that every one can judge for himself
and add to or deduct from the estimate of the
writer.

The diagrams used in these experiments were,
firstly, a series of diagrams drawn by myself, ten
in number, on March 7, together with a single
printed diagram, and seventy-five in number, on
subsequent occasions; and secondly, diagrams
drawn (not in the same room, in order to avoid
subconscious perception of the character of the
drawing) by the agent. This second class was of
course liable to the objection that, apart from a
diagram-habit, a series of similar diagrams might
be drawn by both agent and percipient owing
to a train of ideas being suggested by external
circumstances. At the same time it should be
remembered, in estimating the value of such
experiments, that possibility is not probability, far
less certainty. The drawings made by the agents
were shut up in a large diary, before they entered
the room, and I satisfied myself in each case that
the diagram remained in the book until the agent

was seated behind the screen. The other diagrams, termed $\frac{B}{1}$, $\frac{B}{2}$, etc., were in a box until the commencement of the experiments and were, except in the fifth experiment, drawn from the box at random. From the third trial onwards on March 7 the success and failure was known to the percipient as well as the agent, and the diagram was shown in each case as soon as the individual experiment was ended. The percipient usually closed her eyes until she got an impression, and then reproduced it in pencil on numbered sheets of paper. Each experiment took from a minute and a half for the first set to two minutes for ten others, including the drawing of the diagrams.

Turning to the individual trials on March 7, at 19, Buckingham Street, with Mrs. Verrall as percipient, Miss P. as agent and N. W. Thomas as recorder, we find a slight resemblance in the first, and a stronger resemblance in the fourth experiment; the sixth was completely right; in the third only one of the tails has got into the picture, and that separated from the main portion; the agent remarked afterwards she felt as if she must draw a circle round the diagram; in the fifth experiment I accidentally exposed diagram $\frac{B}{6}$ in sight of the percipient, and she said, " Give me that

[PLATE III.

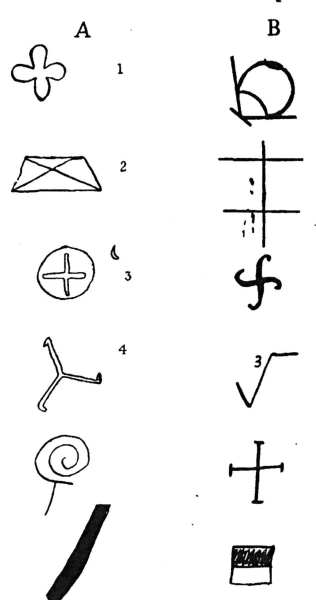

A

1

2

3

4

B

3

TRIALS ON MARCH 7TH.

A. MRS. VERRALL'S DRAWINGS.

B. DIAGRAMS USED BY AGENT.

[*Reduced to one-half.*]

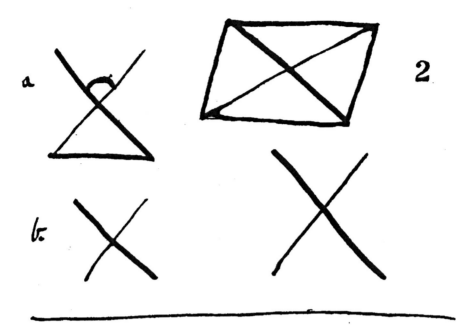

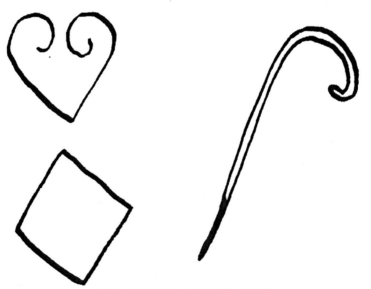

[Plate IV.

B.2

a

2

b.

B.4

TRIALS ON MARCH 7TH.

B 2. 1. *a, b.* MISS P.'S DRAWINGS.   2. DIAGRAMS USED BY AGENTS.

B 4. 1. a, b.   DO   2. DIAGRAM USED BY AGENT.

[*Same size as original.*]

To face p. 145.

one "; I gave her, however, $\frac{B}{4}$; the diagram [1] reproduced was, however, $\frac{B}{6}$, and it can hardly be regarded as accidental that the agent had seen it. The second experiment is virtually a failure, save that the reproduction includes only straight lines and is roughly rectangular, like the diagram.

Miss P. now took Mrs. Verrall's place and the diagrams were drawn by the agents as before described. The first experiment was a failure. In the second [2] a portion of the diagram $\frac{B}{2}$ was given correctly; Mrs. Verrall had numbered it, before entering the room, and enclosed the number in a circle; she said subsequently she felt sure this would be a bother; possibly it may account for the small circle near the cross of the diagonal. Unknown to the percipient, I took from the box diagram $\frac{B}{2}$ and tried a duplex experiment; Miss P. remarked, " I can see two things," and was told to draw them both. The third trial resulted in a reproduction that seems obviously an after image

[1] For $\frac{B}{6}$, see Pl. VII. The series is reproduced on Pl. III.

[2] The figures marked *a* and *b* are Miss P.'s reproductions; the figure marked 2 is Mrs. Verrall's and the last one is $\frac{B}{2}$.

L

from 1 and 2. The fourth experiment had a curious issue; instead of taking a second diagram, I looked, without telling the percipient, at Mrs. Verrall's diagram, and then turned to get a diary as a book-rest for Mrs. Verrall; the first reproduction contained the diagram in duplicate, the reversal of one of the images, as seen by the percipient suggests that the phenomenon of reversal depends on some peculiarity in the agent; it is not impossible that the second refers to the diary, but no stress can be laid on this. The fifth experiment was as good as a failure. For trials 2 and 4 see Pl. IV.

The next set of four trials with Miss P. as agent were virtually all failures. A sickle shaped figure in the first was a reproduction of a portion of the diagram, and in the third experiment the idea present in my mind of a long-tailed cat seated and seen from behind may have influenced the result (a mushroom was drawn), but the resemblance is, in any case, very slight.

On March 24 a further series of 50 with the same ladies as agent and percipient was tried. The diagrams, 75 in number, were made up of the ten previously used and 65 additional ones drawn by N. W. Thomas in the interval. Except in the trials from 31 to 50, the recorder saw the diagram which he handed to the agent, after drawing it at random from the box. Miss P. was the first per-

PLATE V.]

A.

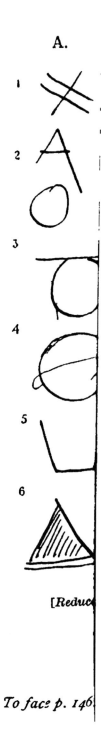

[Reduc

cipient. The first two reproductions were failures; the third was nearly right, and the fourth merely an improvement on the third and quite unconnected with the actual diagram. The fifth was wrong; the sixth, of which Mrs. Verrall's impression was " A V with a tail and something looking at it," was partly right; the seventh and eighth were failures; the ninth resulted in a preliminary failure—no impression; a duplex trial was then made and a double impression resulted, one of which resembled one of the diagrams; in the tenth a duplex trial was again made and resulted in a single impression, a part of which bore a slight resemblance to the diagram. For this series see Pl. V.[1]

In one series of 10 both Miss P. and Mrs. Verrall acted as percipients, and N. W. Thomas as agent. In the first of the series both were, independently, partly right, but Miss P. alone met with further success. On the whole the 60 trials, six of which were duplex, resulted in a much lower percentage of success than the former series, the results being: completely right, 0; half right or more, 6; partly right, 11; some resemblance, 8; and complete

[1] This first series is reproduced as a specimen taken at random to show the general character of the impressions, and the approximation between diagram and impression and to show also that slight resemblances are not unduly emphasized. 3 and 6 were counted a single success between them, 9 as partly R and 10 as some resemblance.

failures, 41.   In two cases postponed successes were obtained, the diagram not having been seen by the percipient in the meantime nor mentioned.

The net result of the two series was: Right, 4; half right or more, 8; partly right, 13; some resemblance, 9; wrong, 50 out of 84 trials, including 8 duplex experiments, of which one was completely successful.

At the close of the trials an experiment on novel lines was made.   Both Miss P. and Mrs. Verrall are good visualizers and reproduce their visualizations easily.   Laying a watch with a second hand upon my table, I asked them to draw their mental pictures for the next five minutes, which I would mark by calling out at the close of each.   In the fifth minute, without saying anything to either, I took two diagrams with the intention of influencing them.   Mrs. Verrall drew in succession (1) a nonsense word (? English), (2) three Greek words, (3) a circle and an H with a labyrinthine figure between, (4) two Latin words, and (5) a house.

Miss P.'s drawings are reproduced on Pl. VI.

Although the resemblance may not be very close it can hardly be denied that a resemblance is present, to the second of the above figures especially.   It should be noted that nothing resembling them had been drawn previously, the

[PLATE VI.

TRIAL ON MARCH 24TH.
Figs. 1—5. MISS P.'S DRAWINGS.
B. 1, 2. DIAGRAMS USED BY AGENT.

[PLATE VII.

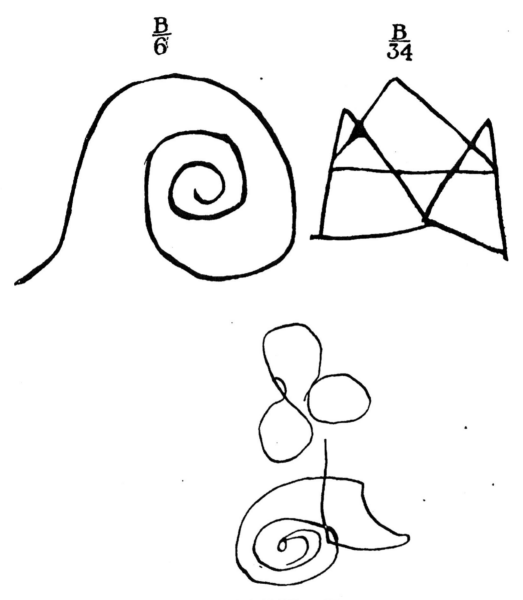

$\dfrac{B}{6'}$ $\dfrac{B}{34}$

TRIAL ON APRIL 23RD.

$\dfrac{B}{6'}$ $\dfrac{B}{34}$. DIAGRAMS USED BY AGENT.

MISS T.'S AUTOMATIC DRAWING.

[Extreme width of original drawing 4⅛ in.]

To face p. 149.

crescents and semicircles being quite different from the last of the above figures.

At 20, Hanover Square, a series of trials with diagrams were made on the same days as the experiments already described, the percipients being Miss T., Miss P. and Mrs. M. The two latter drew their impressions on numbered slips of paper, as already described, but Miss T.'s reproductions were mainly automatic. The main difficulty with automatic drawings was found to be that the motor impulse was not exhausted, when a drawing was completed, but that the hand continued to make unnecessary movements which completely obscured the original reproduction. Partly as a result of this only one conspicuous success was chronicled.

On April 23, 1903, Mr. W. W. Baggally was agent, Miss Keates, shorthand note-taker, and N. W. Thomas, recorder and director of the experiments for the first two trials, both of which were, unknown to the percipient and the original agent, duplex; the second of these resulted in a drawing here reproduced with facsimiles of the original Pl. VII. The resemblance of the upper portion to the three triangles may be called in question, but the identity of the scroll with the diagram in the hands of the agent (N. W. Thomas) is unmistakable. Two later trials resulted in failures.

On May 6 three further duplex trials were made, Miss T. being percipient in one room and W. W. Baggally and G. Musgrove, agents, in another. The first objects were a crescent and a star. Miss T. began by drawing three or four crescents, and then as usual tailed off into meaningless scrawls. In the next experiments, O and S, capital letters, were the objects. Miss T. drew a line some two inches long, ending in a circle three quarters complete, then a figure shaped like a 9; these may have been attempts to give the O. The next two diagrams were $\dfrac{B^1}{7}$ and $\dfrac{B}{8}$. Miss T. between two straight lines drew first a square, then a smaller irregular closed figure, then a very distinct 8. Each experiment seems, therefore, to have been partially successful, and it is worthy of note that the successes, such as they were, were with the diagrams in the hands of one percipient, Mr. Baggally, with whom she was trying another series of long distance experiments.

On May 13, four similar single experiments resulted in failure, Miss T.'s pencil tracing nothing intelligible.

Four trials with numbers were then made, N. W. Thomas and W. W. Baggally, in one room, being

[1] A square

co-agents with numbers 20 and 18 for the first experiment. Miss T. drew an O preceded by a 1 (?); in the next, 48 and 21 being the numbers, 19 was drawn; in the next, 19 being the number, 84 was drawn, and in the last nothing intelligible. In the first two trials it was 6 to 4 against any rough figure being the same as one of those in the agent's hands and 4 to 3 on one of the two figures being the same. As a matter of fact, in the first trial the two figures were each the same as one in the hands of each agent. In the second one figure was right; in other words chance alone explains the two combined. In the third the figures of the second experiment were given in reversed order, possibly a postponed effect from the previous trial.[1]

On April 25 twenty trials, four of them duplex, were made with Miss P. as percipient. Of the first series of ten, two were partly right and one of these appeared again, as a postponed effect, in the following experiment. Of the next ten the first three were with capital letters; there was one complete success; in the first trial in taking out the letter D, N. W. Thomas accidentally saw the letter B, and this was reproduced by the percipient, making what was really a success in one element of a duplex trial.

[1] No results were communicated till the end of a series where the agent and percipient were in different rooms.

Of the seven diagrams two were partly right and in one case there was another unintended success of a kind. The object was Ω; this reappeared as O and inside it 73; the number of the diagram was $\frac{B}{37}$, and it can hardly be a mere coincidence that the number written down was 73.

On May 1, eleven trials were made with Miss P. as percipient, N. W. Thomas agent, and J. G. Piddington recorder. Three of these were half right or better, and one of these reappeared as a postponed effect. In two further cases there was some resemblance. In the fifth experiment the object of which was ε the agent tried glimpsing it by blinking his eyes rapidly (this was recorded before the result of the experiment was known) and the percipient drew a series of C, a result that can hardly be due to chance. In twenty further trials with two percipients little success was attained, there being a resemblance traceable in five cases only.

The net result of the 160 trials recorded here is as follows: right, 5; half right or more, 9; partly right, 16; and some resemblance, 16. The complete failures were 114 in number, the postponed successes, 3. The duplex experiments were in one case completely successful and in several cases partially successful. How far, if at all, these results exceed expectation it is difficult to say. It is clear that much depends on the extent to which half and partial successes might be brought into connexion with other diagrams than those actually used in the experiment. In proportion as this was possible, the excess of successes, if any, is diminished. It seems, however, clear that five complete successes out of 160 is considerably in excess of expectation, and if that is so the evidence for telepathy cannot but be strengthened even by the very moderate results here set forth.

CHAPTER IX

Card Experiments

*Independent variables—Trials in same room—
Postponed successes—Cyclic guessing—Trials
in different rooms.*

In experiments with cards and numbers statistical
evaluation of the expectation is possible. In some
respects experiments with cards offer advantages
over those with numbers. We have in a playing
card a combination of two independent elements,
which are perhaps, however, sufficiently closely
combined in the thoughts of the average unre-
generate human being as to be little more difficult
to grasp than the simple number. When we have
independent variables combined in this way, we
have, it is clear, a method of discovering whether
any unknown cause is operating which is, on the
whole, more certain, where the excess above expectation is small, than where we have only one
element to be guessed. If experience shows that
the tendency is for success or failure in guessing
the two variables to go together, or, in other words,
if the good " number " days are also good " suit "
days, we may reasonably conclude that there is

154

a common cause at work, whether it be the ordinary operation of the sensory perceptions, or hyperæsthesia, or telepathic influence of some sort. On the other hand, the absence of this concomitant variation can hardly be regarded as absolutely conclusive evidence against telepathy, for it is clear that, in so far as the agent is unable to or does not grasp the card as a whole, but needs to deal with the number and the suit as independent factors, the supposition no longer holds good on which was based the expectation of concomitant variation.

Two thousand and eighty single (i.e. with one percipient) trials took place at the rooms of the S.P.R.; I took part as percipient in 1,339, and as agent in 585; in the remainder, 156 in number, Mr. Piddington was the agent. In analysing the results, which were not in themselves much, if at all, above expectation, I hit upon a method of treating the figures, analogous indeed to that used by Mrs. Sidgwick, inasmuch as I separated the good series from the bad, but even, as far as I went, a step further and considered the possibility of another element, that of postponed successes. The trials took place in batches of thirteen or twenty-six, in one series with agent and percipient in the same room, in another and longer set with agent and percipient in different rooms. The

signal was in the second set given by ringing an
electric bell; communication was otherwise difficult or impossible, the rooms being separated by a
store room; access to both was from a landing,
but the doors were separated by some ten feet and
were at right angles to one another so that no
sound, unless of the nature of a thump on the door
or the floor, was audible from one room to the other
when both doors were closed.

The analysis of series A, which was conducted
with agent and percipient in the same room, the
card drawing being written down after the guess,
but not told to the percipient till the end of the series
of thirteen, showed that there was in my own case
a marked tendency for the card itself, and a less
marked tendency for the suits and numbers of
the card drawn for one experiment to appear in
the guess following, a result which may, without
prejudging the cause to which that success was due,
be termed a postponed success. It suggested itself
as a possible explanation of this phenomenon that
I was able to interpret unconsciously the sound of
the pencil and thus discover the card. On the
other hand, it was not impossible that the result
was due not to ordinary sense perception of un-
usual delicacy, but to another means of transmission which we describe provisionally as telepathy.
With a view to testing these hypotheses, I tried

another long series with agent and percipient in different rooms. An analysis of the results of series C in the main and in detail, distributing them according to success or failure in naming cards, numbers, and suits, showed, however, that, so far from postponed successes being distributed according to the same law as in the previous series, the relation was in many cases just the reverse. Into this I go more in detail below, as well as into the real meaning of the successes in series A.

A few experiments were tried with two percipients. Here, too, there is a manifest advantage in using in an experiment two independent variables. This advantage is, however, largely neutralized, so far as the production of direct evidence of thought transference goes, by the possibility of thought transference between the percipients as well as to them. When the trials are further analysed to show in what cases, if any, there were postponed successes, we have a considerable complication. In fact, if thought transference takes place at all, it may be from the agent A to both the percipients, B and C, or to either of them, or from B to C, or vice versa, directly; there may also be thought transference from A to B, or C, or both, or from B to C, or C to B, which results in a postponed success; and direct and postponed successes may obviously be combined in more than one way.

On the whole, therefore, this method of experimentation does not seem to promise to give with cards as satisfactory results as have been attained with diagrams or other objects where the individual trial can be prolonged until the subconscious image, if any, has come to the surface. At the same time, even though it may be difficult to evaluate the probabilities, it can hardly be denied that a close relation displayed between the cards' drawn and the guesses of one of the percipients on the one hand, and the guesses of the other percipient on the other hand, may constitute effective evidence in favour of thought transference.

In the 663 experiments tried with the agent and percipient in the same room, the card being written down after the percipient had made his guess, N. W. Thomas was percipient in 442 with Miss Larminie as agent, and the relation was reversed in the remainder. The agent sat behind an American roll top desk, in such a position that no reflections could give a clue to the card drawn; as an additional precaution the fronts of the Globe-Wernicke bookcases were usually drawn up; but it would have been impossible in any case to see anything in them, even if the eyes of the percipient were not, as was usually the case, closed while the experiments were going on. The total successes were in the two cases as follows—

Percipients	Trials.	Direct Successes.			Postponed Successes.			Remarks.[1]		
		Cards.	Nos.	Suits.	Cards.	Nos.	Suits.	Cards.	Nos.	Suits.
							Successes. Expectation. Figure of merit.			
N. W. Thomas. All days.	442	$\frac{4}{8}$	$\frac{31}{35}$	$\frac{88}{100}$	$\frac{4}{8}$	$\frac{85}{85}$	$\frac{107}{107}$	×	×	o
		−50	−11	−12	+85	+13				
Bad days.[2] Cards below expectation · · ·	364							×	o	o
Nos. · · ·	260							×	×	×
Suits · · ·	312							×	×	×
Good days. Nos. above expectation · · ·	156							o	×	o
Suits · · ·	130							o	o	o

Where the result on all days differs from expectation by more than 10 per cent., the difference and direction of the variation is given in percentage by the number and sign below the fraction expressing the relation of successes to expectation.

The series shorter than 52 are omitted except in the table for all days.

[1] Where the plus in direct successes corresponds to a minus in postponed successes, which I term the *inverse* relation, the column contains a ×; where one of the factors is normal (indeterminate relation), the column contains a o; where both successes and postponed successes are plus or minus, the column contains a 1 (simple relation). Where both are normal, the column is blank (neutral relation).

[2] Days on which the numbers were normal or subnormal.

Percipient.	Trials.	Direct Successes.			Postponed Successes.			Remarks.		
		Cards.	Nos.	Suits.	Cards.	Nos.	Suits.	Cards.	Nos.	Suits.
V. Larminie. All days.	221	$\frac{4}{4}$ +50	$\frac{24}{4}$ +47	$\frac{48}{88}$ −15	$\frac{4}{4}$	$\frac{18}{4}$ −19	$\frac{62}{81}$ +24	0	×	×
Bad days. Cards	156									×
Nos.	52								0	×
Suits	156							×	×	×
Good days. Cards	52							×	×	×
Nos.	156							×	×	×
Suits	52									0

In each of these tables the numerator of the fraction shows the actual, the denominator the probable number of successes.

It is a striking and important fact that, as this statement shows, the successes and failures in direct results corresponded to failures and successes in postponed results, and that the deviation from expectation was greatest in cards in the one case, and in cards and numbers in the other case, whereas in suits it was, though very perceptible, far less marked. It must be remembered that the chance of guessing the suit correctly is one in four and that there is a natural tendency to guess suits in a kind of cycle; in other words, that whereas pure chance would, in the long run, show a fairly even distribution of choice among the suits, the effect of the voluntary element in the selection is to make the difference less perceptible in short series than they otherwise would be. If, for example, hearts has been guessed, one of the other three suits is more likely to be guessed, to an extent impossible to estimate, in the next trial, and, to a less extent, one of the two remaining ones in the following trial, and so on. The effect of this is, where the series is on the whole unsuccessful, to render a postponed success more probable than if chance alone regulated the choice of a suit. On the other hand, it tends to eliminate any effect due to telepathy, inasmuch as the selection is not made at random, so far as the percipient's conscious action is concerned; this would only happen if in

M

each case the percipient had forgotten, or could
dismiss from his mind, the previous guess, and this
is naturally very difficult where each trial does not
occupy more than thirty seconds. It seems clear
that, so far as direct successes are concerned, the
result is to diminish the chances of success, if there
is any telepathic element; the case is less clear
in the case of postponed successes, but probably
the chances of success are, after a previous failure,
increased; for, quite apart from any telepathic
element, the chance of guessing right is nearer
1 in 3 than 1 in 4, and the cyclic tendency would
not conflict perceptibly with any telepathic impulse to choose the right suit. An examination
of the more detailed analysis shows that the same
law holds good both for good·and bad days as for
the results as a whole. Taking cards and numbers,
as well as suits, save where the results, in both cases,
are equal to the expectation or differ from it only
by unity, and 5 of the 9 cases of this are on N. W.
T.'s good days, the same relation is found; or, in
other words, in 24 cases out of 33, direct successes
are in inverse proportion to postponed successes; in
the remaining 9 cases we cannot speak of the result
as either a success or a failure, for the simple reason
that it is practically just what chance alone would
give.

Now it is apparent that what has been said of

the cyclic nature of the guesses applies practically
only to suits.   There may be a tendency to guess
all the numbers once in each thirteen trials, but
the influence on any individual guess is indefinitely
smaller than in the case of suits; in the case of
cards this tendency is almost non-existent, for one
remembers but seldom whether any particular card
has been guessed during the series of 52.   If, therefore, no other cause can be traced for the correlation
between direct and postponed successes and failures
in this series of trials, the results are *prima facie*
evidence in favour of telepathy, in spite of the fact
that the totals do not, except in two cases, markedly
exceed expectation.

It has been suggested above that hyperæsthesia,
or at any rate unsuspected delicacy of normal
perception, may have operated to cause the plus of
postponed successes.   It is clearly no far-fetched
hypothesis that the ear could detect and interpret
the difference of the sound of the pencil according
to the name of the suit that was being written.
But it must be noted that it is precisely in suits,
when on this hypothesis the result should be most
marked, that the difference between expectation
and result is smallest.   In the case of numbers
which would only be readily apprehended in the
way suggested above after considerably more
practice than in the case of suits, the results are

actually more striking than in the case of suits. It seems, therefore, difficult to explain the facts on this theory.

In the second place, even if this view were satisfactory in the cases where the postponed successes exceed expectation, it could not account for the cases where the inverse relation is still found, but with the plus on the side of the direct successes; these cases make up 8 of the 24 cases in which the results deviated from expectation; 7 of these refer to the trials when Miss Larminie was percipient.

Finally the theory of hyperæsthesia does not explain the very considerable plus in the case of cards when N. W. T. was percipient. It is clear that if this plus is due to independent perception of the two elements—the number and the suit —by auditory means, there is no reason why they should appear more often conjoined than apart. The number of cases is, it is true, small, but, so far as the evidence goes, it seems to show that the cause which produced the plus of successes in cards was not independent perception of the elements; for then we should expect a far higher proportion of successes in the elements disjoined than was actually the case, viz., 13 per cent. and 5 per cent. On the other hand it is not difficult to understand how telepathic influence might bring about the result. Postponed successes in cards, due, *ex hypothesi,* to a specially strong telepathic influence which takes some time to emerge, would naturally tend to be more numerous proportionately than successes in the individual elements; where the telepathic influence is selective and transmits or transmits strongly only one of the two elements, it would, perhaps, be in itself weaker and therefore less likely to operate; for whatever makes for a strong impulse would normally make for an impulse embracing both elements.

I now turn to the experiments, distinguished as Series C, in which the agent and percipients were in different rooms. The *modus operandi* was as follows: The agent was, as a rule, in the secretary's room, and the percipient in the library; the second percipient, if there was one, was in the store room between. The agent, having rung the electric bell as a signal, drew a card from one pack, and noted it on a numbered sheet; for the second card another pack was utilised, to ensure adequate shuffling of the cards; notice was given by the agent in each case by ringing the bell. The pace of the trials was therefore independent of the rate at which the percipient got impressions and was usually decided on beforehand when the agent was able to shuffle, draw, and record faster than the percipient got an impression.

The analysis of Series C is as follows—

Percipient.	Trials.	Direct Successes.			Postponed Successes.			Remarks.[2]		
		Cards.	Nos.	Suits.	Cards.	Nos.	Suits.	Cards.	Nos.	Suits.
N. W. Thomas.	897	+12			+18	+10	−9	―	o	o
Good days. Cards	325							―	x ―	x
Nos.	377							―	―	o
Suits	312							―	o	
Bad days. Cards	572							o o o	x o o	o o o
Nos.	520									
Suits	585									
V. Larminie.	520	+30		+16		+7		p̣	o	―
Good days. Cards	208							― o	o x	o ―
Nos.	104									
Suits[1]										
Bad days. Cards	360							―	o o	― o
Nos.	416									

[1] Suits were normal on one day, on all other days above.

[2] For explanation of Signs see page 159.

The inverse relation of successes and failures is, as the foregoing table shows, preserved in not a single case out of six in the results as a whole; in two cases the relation is reversed, and both sides are above expectation; in the three cases one of the factors to be compared is normal, and the remaining one is, in each case, above normal, and in one case both are normal. The consideration of the results as a whole therefore lends no support to the theory of thought transference.

If we now take the detailed analysis, we find the inverse relation in 4 cases out of 30, the simple relation (both above) in 8, both are normal in 2, and the remaining 16 are indeterminate, one factor being normal and the other six times above and ten times below normal. Here again we find no support for the hypothesis of thought transference, so far as such analysis can throw any light on the matter. We may, however, note that on N. W. T.'s bad days the inverse relation is found on four occasions and the indeterminate on five. In Series A the bad days seemed in the case of the same percipient to be accounted for, if there was any telepathic element, by the slow emergence of the impulse. That being so we seem to have in the bad days of Series C a continuation of the same phenomenon, though here it seems to be on the whole more prominent in the numbers, the cards being in one case above normal, and the suit in two cases, when one of the other elements was below normal.

For comparison with Series A I have given the percentages above and below the normal. In only five cases out of twelve are they the same as in the previous trials. In both N. W. T. got postponed cards and numbers above the normal; V. L. on the other hand got cards postponed just above the normal. In five cases the results in one or other series did not differ from the normal by more than 10 per cent., a variation well within the normal limits in a short series; in the remaining cases the figures (for cards) varied from the normal, on small numbers, by no more than two, and may consequently be neglected.

It is perhaps idle to suggest causes for a variation which may be due to chance alone, but it seems desirable to point out the two series were carried out under somewhat different conditions, quite apart from the fact that in Series A, agent and percipient were in the same room. In the first series the signal for the next trial was a guess by the percipient, in Series C the agent was able to communicate with the percipient, but not *vice versâ;* consequently, the series once started, the pace was out of the percipient's control and the knowledge of this fact, no less than the different speed at which the two series were taken, may well have had some influence on the results.

In considering the evidence from direct and postponed successes, it should not be overlooked that the same item may appear in both if two suits, numbers or cards drawn in succession are the same. The results cannot therefore be added. In Series A (N. W. T.) there were 24 coincidences of this sort, in Series C (N. W. T.), 28; in Series A (V.L.), 18, and in Series C, 34.

It should also be noted that on each of the eleven days on which Miss Larminie was percipient the suits only once fell below expectation, and that in a short series.

It may be well to call attention here to a factor which tends to reduce any excess of successes. This is the fact, already noticed in another connexion, that the percipient, as a rule, seldom guesses suits in pairs; that is to say, that hearts having been guessed, the next guess is more likely to be clubs, spades, or diamonds, whereas if chance alone operated, or, if the percipient forgot in each case the previous guess, each of the four suits would be equally likely. The extent of this tendency naturally differs with the individual. In the case of Miss Larminie a pair was guessed on an average four times in 52 trials, in the case of N. W. Thomas only three times, against expectation, if chance alone operated, of 6 or 7 pairs and one or two trios, with a quartet in every 100 trials.

The result of this is manifest.   While it does not reduce the chances below 1 in 4, it leads to reduce any excess above 1 in 4.   If for example, to take an extreme case, some cause operated to make half instead of one-fourth of the guesses successful, so long as this cyclic tendency did not make its appearance, there would be 26 successes in 52 trials; three or four pairs would be guessed correctly. The cyclic tendency would reduce the number of pairs correctly guessed, if the law of averages were strictly adhered to, by one-half or more in the two cases under consideration.   This would mean that the total successes out of fifty-two trials would be less by two.   As a matter of fact, in the 2,000 odd trials the coincidences between guessed doublets and drawn doublets, which should, allowing for cyclic guessing, have been about sixteen in number, were actually only four, a variation for which I cannot suggest any explanation.

The net result is, of course, not large; but the influence, whatever it was, which caused the discrepancy, has clearly reduced the number of successes by about 3 per cent.   Unless, or until, this negative result is explained as not due to chance alone, the probability of thought transference as an operative cause in the series we have been considering is diminished; for if chance alone can produce such a result in a fairly long series, it may well account for the successes.

I now turn to the consideration of the trials with two percipients; the analysis, more complicated than in the case of a single percipient, is as follows :—

Dec. 13. Percipient.	Trials.	Successes from Agent		Cross Successes Postponed.					
		Direct.	Postponed.	Direct.	Mrs. V.		Miss V.	N. W. T.	
					to Miss V.	to N.W.T.	to Mrs. V.		
Mrs. Verrall [1]	26	3/7	8	0	2	3	2	4	Suits
		1/2	I	I	I	I	0	I	Nos.
		o	o	o	o	o	o	I	Cards
					Miss V.		N.W.T.	Mrs. V.	
					to Mrs. V.	to N.W.T.	to Miss V.		
Miss Verrall [2]	39	5/7	1.1	5	2	5	8	2	Suits
		3/4	I	I	0	I	3	I	Nos.
		o	o	o	o	I	3	o	Cards
					N. W. T.		Mrs. V.	Miss V.	
					to Mrs. V.	to Miss V.	to N.W.T.		
N. W. Thomas	39	18/8	6	5	4	8	5	3	Suits
		3	4	0	I	3	I	I	Nos.
		o	I	o	I	3	o	o	Cards

[1] Agent in one series.
[2] Agent in two series.

The fractions in the column of direct successes from the agent show the proportion of successes to expectation.

Jan. 14. Percipient.	Trials.	Successes from Agents.		Cross Successes Postponed.			Suits Nos. Cards
		Direct.	Post-poned.	Direct.	L. to T.	T. to L.	
Miss L.[1] Mrs. G.	26 26	8 0 0 4 2 0	7 0 0 9 3 1	13 2 1	6 3 1	6 3 1	Suits Nos. Cards

Feb. 2.[2]		Direct.	Post-poned.	Direct.	R. to T.	T. to R.	Suits Nos. Cards
Miss R.[3]	13	3 2 0	4 2 1	1 1 0	2 2 0	5 1 1	Suits Nos. Cards

					H. to T.	T. to H.	Suits Nos. Cards
Mrs. H.[4]	39	16 5 1	7 3 0	10 6 3	9 3 1	9 3 2	Suits Nos. Cards

					T. to R.	to H.	R. to T.	H. to T.	Suits Nos. Cards
N. W. T.	30	10 6 2	10 3 1	11 7 3	5 1 1	9 3 2	2 2 0	9 3 1	Suits Nos. Cards

Feb. 19.					H. to L.	L. to H.	
Miss Larminie[5] Mrs. H.	47 47	14 3 1 16 3 1	20 3 0 15 2 1	13 4 2	1 0 0	13 1 0	

[1] J. G. Piddington, agent.
[2] For a copy of the record in a portion of this experiment, see p. 210.
[3] Agent in three series.
[4] Agent in one series.
[5] Agent, N. W. Thomas.

Percipient.	Trials.	Successes from Agent.		Cross Successes.		
		Direct.	Postponed.	Direct.	L. to R	R. to L.
Miss R.[1]	26	8	3			
		4	3		7	6
		1	0	4		
Miss Larminie	26	8	8	1	3	0
		1	1	1	1	0
		0	6			

In these five sets of trials, which are not selected in any way, but constitute the whole of those made with two percipients, the direct successes from agent to either of the percipients were 6 cards, 32 numbers and 109 suits in 406 trials, a result only slightly above chance in the case of the two latter. If we look at the direct correspondence between the two percipients, we find that, in spite of our unsuccessful series, the percipients guessed the same card 7 times in 190 trials, as against expectation 3 or 4. More striking still are the results where N. W. Thomas acted as one of the percipients. Analysing the two series, 91 trials in all, we find that while the direct correspondences were 16, 7, 3 with numbered cards, the postponed successes of the second percipient, in other words the guesses which showed a relation to N. W. T.'s preceding guess, were 26 suits, 8 numbers and 7 cards, as against expectation 21, 6 or 7, 1 or 2.

[1] Agent, N. W. Thomas.

There is an obvious danger in selecting in a short series the performances of one agent (or possible agent), however much they may be above chance, and founding on them an argument. But if thought transference is a fact, we might expect to find considerable variation; and one agent is likely to be, in the long run, considerably more successful than another. In the present case the selection of results seems to be justified by the other series. Leaving out of account the successes just mentioned, in the 626 trials where N. W. T. acted as agent, the successes in cards were 16 as against expectation 12, a percentage less marked indeed than that in the duplex trials, but still not inconsiderable; the suits were slightly above chance, and the numbers showed a plus of 8 or 16 per cent. The totals for all trials in which N. W. Thomas acted as agent are 23 cards, 64 numbers, and 185 suits, showing an excess of 67 per cent., 16 per cent., and 3 per cent. respectively.

CHAPTER X

The net result—Future investigation

NOTHING is more difficult than to sum up the net result of experiments so diverse in their nature and outcome as the various series described above. With the exception of the card series, none of the trials embraced any great number of separate experiments, and in none of the brief series is the possibility of chance coincidence excluded, however improbable it may appear in certain cases. The results of the card experiments, on the other hand, are hardly sufficiently decisive for it to be possible to base any conclusion on them.

I am less disposed to sum up the miscellaneous experiments here published for the first time, as it is, *a priori*, certain that no argument based upon them is likely to affect any one's convictions. Those who are satisfied that telepathy " and all that nonsense " is impossible, will not be moved, even if an angel come from heaven. Those who hold that the mass of evidence is yet too small, or that in many of the previous trials the conditions have not been such as to exclude undesired perturbations, will not find in the present contribution matter of sufficient weight to turn the scale in favour of telepathy. Perhaps those who are already convinced that thought transference is a fact will think me unduly exacting, when I demand more evidence and especially more recent evidence than any which the Society for Psychical Research has put before us. I should therefore run the risk of offending all my readers and pleasing none. Not only so; I should probably fail to please myself, if not at the moment, at any rate, after an interval for reflection.

I adopt, therefore, the safer plan of leaving my readers to make up their minds on the subject of these experiments for themselves. If I venture to express my own conviction on the subject, it is that much more effort, and, in particular, much more systematic effort, is needed before we can safely assert that telepathy is a proved[1] fact. When we have arrived at that point our task is only begun. No inquiry can lay claim to be scientific which expresses its results in general terms when it can give them in precise terms. The study of heredity

[1] By this I mean proved by direct experiment. When we take into account crystal gazing and the spontaneous cases, the weight of evidence in favour of telepathy is considerably greater. For a discussion of the latter cases see *Phantasms of the Living* and the census (*Proc. S.P.R.*, x. 14, sq.). Crystal gazing is dealt with in another volume of this series.

and other biological questions has become a question of statistics, and psychical research must also be made a question of statistics if further conclusions are to be based on the results.

The statistical method has of course been applied, especially in the case of death-wraiths, which formed the subject of an elaborate statistical inquiry some twelve years ago. It has also been applied to experimental thought transference data, but it has hardly been recognized that the few complete series which have been published are sufficient even to demonstrate the mere fact of telepathy, and, *a fortiori*, for statistical purposes.

Many of the earlier series were not published *in extenso*. Of those which have been published in full, the Brighton experiments depended largely, if not entirely, on the efforts of a single agent. It would be well for the Society for Psychical Research to recognize this and organize further experiments on a large scale before assuming, as its members commonly do in discussions on trance mediumship, that telepathy is a *vera causa*, and not only needs no further demonstration, but may be invoked on any and every occasion, regardless of the fact that, in so doing, a *rôle* is frequently assigned to it which may well stagger the imagination, though no evidence, scientific or otherwise, has ever been presented for the telepathic power in the extreme form in which it

is invoked, to explain away experiments more readily
explained on a spiritistic hypothesis.

The telepathic or some other non-spiritistic explanation may well be the true one in many, perhaps
in all cases; at present, thanks to the lack of data collected with due precautions, a state of things largely
due to lack of scientific education among spiritualists, and to their want of appreciation of the funda-
mentals of scientific evidence, the supposed proofs
of spiritualism, or in other words of the continued
existence of those who have undergone the change
we call death, are from any standpoint with the least
claim to be called scientific, hardly, if at all, better
founded than those of telepathy, and these, as I
have suggested, are hardly strong enough to bear
the burden put upon them. The evidence for
spiritualism, however, suffers in addition from this
inherent defect, that so long as it is conceivable, if
perhaps improbable, that all the facts on which spiritualists rely, can be explained away by a telepathic
hypothesis; or by some such theory as that put
forward by Dr. Leaf, who holds that the evidence
gathered from the phenomena of trance mediumship
points in the direction of a survival of memory, but
not of personality (in some such way as a phono-
graph preserves the words and the voice, but is not
itself sentient), the extent of the evidence for
spiritualism must remain a matter of doubt, and be

liable to reduction in proportion as we can justly ascribe to telepathy the supercognitive[1] phenomena of trance mediumship.

But it is equally clear that we are by no means entitled to assume the truth of telepathy on insufficient grounds and invoke it on any and every occasion in preference to spiritualistic explanations. Any hypothesis that has the least claim to be called scientific must rest on laws, not on guesses; and in order to have any value in the present case these laws must be formulated with a degree of definiteness that will only be possible after enormous labour.

The Society for Psychical Research was formed to investigate telepathy as well as spiritualism. At present all its energies seem to be directed towards inquiries into trance mediumship, automatic writing, and the like, to the exclusion of the work which should really form the foundation of the whole structure of Psychical Science, the establishment of the theory of telepathy, if true, and its formulation in the most definite terms possible.

Perhaps it may never be possible to formulate a telepathic law in terms like those of the law of gravitation, or to devise such experimental conditions as will enable the student of trance mediums

[1] Supercognition is the acquisition of knowledge by supernormal means. For a glossary of psychical terms see *Proc. S.P.R.* vol. xii.

to say with confidence that his results cannot be explained by telepathy. But, until the effort has been made, no investigation into trance mediumship has the data which can alone enable it to formulate reliable conclusions. In order to justify its existence as a body whose object it is to approach the study of these questions scientifically, the Society for Psychical Research must endeavour to supply these data and again take up the question of thought transference. That other subjects attract a greater share of popular interest is clearly no reason for dropping the inquiry. Still less is absence of success, which appears to have prevented the publication of the trials between 1892 and 1901, a reason for discontinuing them. For it is clear that the smaller the measure of success under rigid conditions, the more probable is it that the conditions in earlier and more successful trials were lacking in some essential particular. It may be added that whatever be the reason for ill-success, it seems desirable to analyze all future records, or at any rate preserve them, for future investigators, a step which has unfortunately been omitted in the past.

Pending organized effort of this kind, much may be done by individuals. My object has been to give an account of experiments in which neither agents nor percipients were in any way selected and which may therefore be taken as a specimen of what any one may hope to accomplish. For if thought transference is ever to be proved, it must be by showing that it is a faculty common to the human race and not one absolutely limited to a few individuals. Reasonably or unreasonably, if thought transference cannot, with sufficient patience and sufficiently delicate methods of analysis, be demonstrated on the *corpus vile*, or rather the *anima vilis*, of the ordinary man, it will for the mass of scientific men remain, at any rate, on the borderland, if not in the limbo of superstitions and delusions.

If a hundred, or five hundred, or five thousand, persons were prepared to try, under proper conditions (a subject to which I return below), experiments of the sort described here, leaving the discussion and analysis to experts, it might be possible, if not to demonstrate thought transference from the results, at any rate to say more definitely than we can at present, whether the ordinary person shows any traces of such a faculty. If the present account, by making it clear that thought transference, contrary to the commonly received opinion, is far from having been experimentally demonstrated, stimulates public interest in the question and induces some of my readers to experiment and submit their results to myself or the S.P.R., I shall have attained my object.

CHAPTER XI

The Ethics of criticism—Problems—Theories—Objections—Mind and Matter—Psychophysical parallelism—The Ignorance of science—Basis of Belief that language conveys ideas

IN the opening chapter I dealt with some of the general objections which are, or have been, from time to time, brought against telepathy and telæs-.thesia; in connexion with the various experiments I have indicated some of the objections which might be raised, and the precautions taken to avoid causes of error. In this chapter, I propose to discuss some of the problems raised by the experiments, so far as they can be regarded as evidence of telepathy and telæsthesia, and to return to some of the objections urged against psychical research. In the first place, I may notice an argument which, irrational as it is, seems to find favour with a certain type of critic. A writer in the *Academy* some year and a half ago, undertook to inquire into the evidence for telepathy, moved thereto by the dictum of Sir Oliver Lodge that he regarded it as scientifically proved; in pursuance of this object he visited the rooms of the Society and spent fully two or three hours in considering the evidence, published and in MSS., and borrowed two volumes containing experiments. We are not immediately concerned with the results of this investigation into the facts; it would, in fact, be difficult to discuss them, inasmuch as the article contained no hint of the reasons which led the author to say that " these experiments prove nothing."

The writer describes me in the article in question as " a representative and official supporter of telepathy." I certainly was not an official supporter of telepathy, inasmuch as belief in telepathy is not a condition of membership, or of office in the Society; whether I was a representative of telepathy I cannot say, as the phrase conveys no meaning to me, any more than the statement that the Secretary of the Royal Society is a representative of the ether or someone else of telegony.

In the course of conversation during his visits to the Society's rooms various questions were discussed in a somewhat fragmentary manner; among other points I was asked how I accounted for the failures. The writer of the article made notes of my words, whether at the time they were uttered or subsequently, he does not state, probably the latter, and gives my explanation in the following terms: " Well, it's exactly the same—mind, I don't say there's the slightest analogy [in the mode of operation]—but it is exactly the same as if you had twenty

Marconi instruments all going at once across the same space." In the above sentence I have interpolated in square brackets words which, if not actually used in the sentence in question, had been used a few moments before. If I had apprehended that Dr. Saleeby, whom I had no reason to suspect of any other than the ordinarily received views on such matter, was going to take surreptitious notes of private conversations, and if I had imagined that a comparatively simple statement, readily capable of being construed to mean something more than the contradiction in terms, which was all Dr. Saleeby could see in it, would not have been understood, I might have abstained from offering an opinion. On the question of failures it may be well to say a few words.

Whether we take the view that telepathy, so far as it is a fact, is due to an intermediate chain of physical causation, or whether, with F. W. H. Myers, we regard it as entirely psychical in its nature, one thing seems certain. That is, that we have no warrant for limiting the influences reaching the brain or the consciousness of the percipient to the physical or psychical energy emitted by the agent. Even if we had not ample experimental evidence that what we may call extraneous ideas are apt to intrude themselves from the minds of those who are not attempting a transference, some examples of which will be found on pp. 141, 151, this would be, *à priori*, highly probable, and the acceptance of this idea in no way involves acceptance of "brain-waves," or any other form of waves, as a theory of thought transference. Interference is equally intelligible on the physical and psychical views of telepathy.

Interference from without is, of course, not the whole explanation. Far more important is the interference due to the ideas and images of the percipient's own mind. As an example of what may well happen in such cases, I may point to the analogous case of dreams evoked, so far as we can see, by an external cause. A friend of mine at Cambridge, dozing one morning after waking, and before getting up, dreamed that he was standing at the window in the Trinity Lodge; he saw a herd of cattle begin to enter the court through the Great Gate; they flowed in a steady stream beneath the Gate Tower, and finally, when the whole of the court, two or three acres in extent, was filled with them, the drover worked his way across and, standing under the window, touched his hat, saying, "Your cattle, sir." Then the dreamer awoke to the fact that his bed-maker was knocking at his door for the second time and saying, "Your kettle, sir," as an intimation that his shaving water was ready. It is difficult to doubt the explanation of the dream, if we accept the story.

Such a development of a simple suggestion is by no means incredible. The important point, however, for our present purpose is that if the dreamer and his bed-maker had been percipient and agent in a thought transference experiment, where the object to be transferred was a kettle, no one but a convinced believer in telepathy would venture to claim the result as a partial success. In the case in question, the fact that the suggestion was a verbal one gives us a key to the development of the dream. In the case of a picture the result may have been less obviously dependent on the initial idea. It is clear that the contribution by the agent will be large or small, in inverse proportion to the contribution of the mind of the percipient. Where the ideas of the agent fail to emerge into the consciousness of the percipient, the result will be a failure.

When indisputable statistical proof is given that the coincidences between the ideas of the agent and the ideas of the percipient are more numerous than chance, including variation due to chance, would give, we cannot, it is clear, attach any importance to failures as an argument against the conclusion drawn from this excess of coincidences. The failures may help to throw light on the laws of thought transference; they cannot any longer throw doubt on the fact. If some one, to take a parallel case, denies the existence of memory (to take an example unthinkable in itself, but convenient as affording a close parallel), on the ground that we do, in fact, forget many more facts of consciousness than we remember, the arguments would hardly be regarded as conclusive. If a child can get no. further in the alphabet than A.B.C. . . . its memory may not be very strong, but it has one. Similarly the proof of thought transference is independent of the existence of failures, though not of the proportion of successes to failures. To this point we return below.

The real problems [1] raised by the experiments in thought transference are very different. Attention has been called, in the preceding pages, to an occasional instance of reversal of the image in a diagram, visualized or drawn automatically. Another case of a rather striking kind, I quote here instead of in the proper place, because the original record has unfortunately been mislaid. In a series with diagrams, I myself being the agent, I interposed a number, using for the purpose one of a set of cloak-room tickets, bought for the purpose; the percipient was unaware that there was any change in the conditions of the experiment, and drew the number 47, which she visualized, in the way described on p. 144, mirror-wise. The experiment

---

[1] Apart, that is, from the primary problem of the nature of the telepathic process, which, for purposes of discussion, I there and elsewhere assume to be a fact.

was tried under the usual conditions, I being behind
my secretaire and the percipient seated with her
back to me in such a position that no reflection from
any bright object was possible.   This was the only
experiment of the kind which I tried.   It resulted
in a complete success, both figures being given correctly, and they were so reproduced as to make it
quite clear that the percipient was unaware that the
visualized image was that of a number.

No statistics on the subject of reversal are available, and they would avail little if we had them.
Except in cases like that just mentioned, where the
reversal strengthens the evidence for thought transference by excluding the more ordinary explanations, the multiplication of cases of reversal is indeed
desirable, but, until we have made some progress
in the explanation of thought transference, comparatively useless for immediate purposes.   As
illustrating the extent to which reversal may take
place, a series of experiments may, however, be
mentioned, the record of which is printed on p. 166
of the first volume of *Proceedings*.   In 37 trials
with one agent and percipient there were no failures
to guess correctly the vertical position of an arrow,
the direction, whether up or down, being also named
correctly in all the 20 trials.   In the 17 trials, however, in which the arrow was in a lateral position,
the right position and direction were named 6 times,

and the right position and wrong direction (reversal) 8 times, and the position was given wrong 3 times.

The conditions seem to have been quite satisfactory, as indeed might have been expected from the names of the experimenters, Messrs. Gurney, Myers, Podmore and Barrett. But it may be pointed out for the benefit of sceptics that if the results were due to indications, conscious or unconscious, there should have been no more difficulty in indicating the direction when the arrow was lateral than when it was vertical.

In the case of reproduction of diagrams by automatic writing, the reversal presents no difficulty; it is paralleled by innumerable cases of mirror-script, and it is unnecessary to assume that reversal in such cases differs from reversal where the writing or drawing is a product solely of the automatist's brain.

The subject of mirror-writing, and seeing, has been discussed by F. W. H. Myers in an early stage of his studies in the subliminal faculty (*Proc. S.P.R.* iii. 39-44). His view is that in automatic writing the action of the right hemisphere of the brain is predominant, because the waking mind, as a rule, makes use of the left hemisphere, and controls it more readily. Dr. Ireland, in a paper on mirror-writing (*Brain*, iv. 366, *sq.*), suggests that the image or impression, or change in the brain tissue, from which the image is formed in the mind of the mirror writer, is reversed like the negative of a photograph; or that if a double image is formed, the images lie in opposite directions.   If this were the case, mirror-writing would be due, he suggests, to the operation of the hemisphere in which the inverse image is formed.

This view, if correct, throws some light on the cases of reversal of the visual image, of which a few examples have been given before. Where the writing is reversed, we have no reason to connect the agent, or rather the conditions under which it is produced, with the result, save so far as we take the view that thought transference is a sub-conscious process in the main, and therefore in all probability, on Myers' hypothesis, connected rather with the right than the left hemisphere. But in the case of the arrow experiments and the duplex experiment mentioned above (p. 146) we have no ground for assuming that the visualization is specially connected with dextro-cerebral [1] processes.   We are by no means bound to look for the cause of the reversal in the percipient; it is equally possible that the image was reversed when it was transmitted; and this view is borne out, so far as a single experiment can bear out any supposition, by the difference be-

[1] That is, processes going on in the right hemisphere of the brain.

tween the images in the duplex experiment, only one of which is reversed. Inasmuch, however, as inversion is not known to occur in hallucinations, which we may also connect with predominant activity of the right side of the brain, we may even go further and argue that all cases of reversal of visualized images must be due to the agent. The subject is, however, exceedingly obscure, and I merely suggest the point as one likely to throw some light on the mechanism of transmission.

In the Sidgwick number-experiments there were a certain number of reversed successes. So far as these were not due to chance we might be tempted to explain them on the same principle as the reversal of diagrams. In an experiment recorded by Mr. Myers (*Proc. S.P.R.* iii. 44) words of three letters were, in two cases, seen reversed, or rather the letters appeared in the field of mental vision in reverse order. These cases differ, however, fundamentally from mirror reversals, in that it is the components which are seen in reversed order and not the whole image which is seen reversed, and it seems safest to conclude that two different sets of causes are at work.

Another problem raised by these experiments is the effect of distance on their success or failure. With the same percipients the proportion of successes at a distance, even where the distance is no more than that between two rooms in the same house, is usually much less considerable than the same proportion in experiments conducted in the same room. In the Sidgwick experiments this was, as we have seen, supposed to be due to the effect of the idea of distance on the mind.[1] Now we have no reason to suppose that conscious effort is necessary or helpful in promoting success. Several cases have been quoted above in which the guess clearly referred to an object seen either by some one else or by the agent, but not intended to be transferred. Unless we suppose that these cases were due to chance alone, a rather sweeping supposition, if we accept thought transference, it is clear that conscious effort has not necessarily anything whatever to do with telepathy so far as the agent is concerned. It is, in fact, quite arguable that the transference takes place when the agent is *not* thinking of the object, card or diagram to be transferred.

We must, therefore, suppose that the ill-success, if it is due to the sense of distance, is due to suggestion operating subconsciously. There is, however,

---

[1] It should not be forgotten, however, that even if clairvoyance proper is not a fact (but little good evidence is available), a considerable number of people seem to be able to guess correctly a considerable proportion of cards drawn at random by themselves and not looked at—a fact not yet thoroughly explained. If the perception is supersensual, the plus of successes in experiments where agent and percipient are in the same room may be one and the same cause. For a discussion of the evidence see p. 43, *ante*.

absolutely nothing in the evidence for spontaneous thought transference to suggest that distance has any effect. Except in so far as the agent or percipi- ent, therefore, believes that distance is a factor, there is no reason to regard it as operative in experiments. The conditions of spontaneous and experimental thought transference are, it is true, very different. In the former cases the transfer- ence is, as a rule, if the evidence collected by the S.P.R. be trustworthy, that of an image of the agent, who is, however, very far from thinking of himself, and is not thinking, in some cases, possibly in a majority of cases, of the percipient. On the other hand, in experimental thought transference, even where no conscious effort is made to transmit ideas, there is always the knowledge that a given person is to be the percipient, and, of necessity, known objects brought expressly before the mind, form the test by which we judge of the success or failure of the experiment. It must not, however, be forgotten that we find connecting links between the two types of phenomena, firstly, in transferences from the agent of ideas not consciously present to his mind and possibly entirely latent, so far as his memory and every-day consciousness are concerned; secondly, in transferences of ideas, equally beneath the surface in most cases, from other than the person who is endeavoring to effect the transference; and thirdly,

in the transference of ideas from an " unconscious
agent," to an " unconscious percipient," that is to
say, where there is no effort either to give or receive.

We may therefore, *prima facie,* regard spontaneous and experimental telepathy as the extreme types
of a single phenomenon. If this is so, we are
justified in saying that distance has in itself no
influence in diminishing the telepathic impulse.
Possibly, if percipient and agent clearly keep this
before their minds, the results of trial at a distance
may improve.

The main purpose of these pages has been to give
an outline of the experimental evidence for thought
transference, and to indicate to those who feel sufficient interest in the question to try experiments
on their own behalf how they can best set about
it.

It will perhaps, however, be not uninteresting to
sketch briefly some of the theories which have been
propounded, by those who accept telepathy as
a fact, in explanation of the transmission of thoughts
and images. These range from von Hartmann's
theory, which makes the Absolute into a telepathic
exchange station for the Universe at large, to the
view of Morin, propounded, it is true, before any of
the experiments here summarized, on the ground
of the so-called community of sensation between

hypnotizer and patient, who accounts for everything by hyperæsthesia.

A theory put forward some twenty years ago by Dr. Baréty, based though it was on entirely insufficient proofs, is worthy of mention, if only for the reason that it, in a way, anticipates the still controverted discovery of Blondlot. The N-rays of the latter had as predecessors the " force neurique rayonnante " of the former, the odic force of Baron Reichenbach and the mesmeric fluid of an earlier day.

Dr. Ochorowicz (*De la Suggestion Mentale*, p. 511) holds that thought remains in the brain, but that, like any other force, it cannot remain isolated; if, however, it passes out of the brain, it does so in another form, just as the chemical energy of the galvanic battery after passing out of the cell is called the electric current. The currents of motor nerves cannot constitute the only dynamic equivalent of the central mechanism.

Mr. Podmore (*Apparitions and Thought Transference*, p. 388) is disposed to suggest " some kind of vibration, propagated somehow through a conjectural medium from an unspecified nerve centre," as an explanation of thought transference.

Professor Flournoy holds that direct action between living beings, independently of the organs of sense, is so in accord with all we know of nature that he would be inclined to suspect its existence quite apart from experimental evidence. He holds that nervous centres must inevitably transmit various undulations which act on similar centres in other skulls.

Sir William Crookes (*Proc. S.P.R.* xii. 348-352) was rash enough in 1898 to court the obloquy which is the certain fate of a scientific man who ventures to go beyond the gospel of science, when, as President of the British Association, he accepted telepathy. Probably, in the eyes of his scientific colleagues, he did little to redeem himself from the reproach of heterodoxy when he propounded a physical theory to account for the obnoxious phenomena. He too holds that thoughts are transmitted by brain waves; and that telepathy is a matter of ether waves of smaller amplitude and greater frequency than those which constitute the X-rays.

In opposition to the views enumerated above, which may be termed " physical," Sir Oliver Lodge upholds the " psychical " view. Mental phenomena, as such, are certainly not physical processes, and physical terms, such as " action at a distance," are probably meaningless and absurd when applied to psychical facts.

F. W. H. Myers in his *Human Personality* (vol. i. p. 245), declares against the vibration theory of Sir William Crookes for reasons which, being drawn from other than experimental telepathic phenomena, do not concern us here.

OBJECTIONS AGAIN

To review all or any of these theories at length is unnecessary in a sketch like the present. It is, however, worth while to point out to those psychologists who ask us for an intelligible physical theory of telepathy, as a condition of considering the evidence, that up to the present no intelligible physical theory of the connexion of mind and matter has been given us by psychologists. If the absence of an intelligible theory, capable of accounting for the facts of the case, is a ground for ignoring the facts, we have no resource but to ignore mental phenomena. If we are not absolute automata, if our mental processes are not the results of an inexorable chain of physical causation, of which the mind is a mere by-product, an epiphenomenon, which has no influence either on its own states or on matter, whether of the brain or otherwise, we may hold (1) that mind and matter interact, and that physical causation is not the only causal relationship in the universe. For clearly if mental states are causes as well as effects, they are either independent of physical causation altogether, or the psychical must be regarded as influencing the physical just as we suppose that the ether influences matter and *vice versâ*. On the other hand, we may hold (2) that mind can influence matter, but that there is no reciprocal action; organized matter is necessary to mind in order to provide it with a means of communicating, without uncertainty, with other minds, but it functions only as a transmitter, and has no more influence on the thought than has the telephone on the voice or ideas of the person who uses it (those cases excluded in which it excites him to use bad language).

Whether these views are true or not, one thing is certain, and that is, that they explain nothing; it cannot, in fact, be claimed that they are theories at all; they are mere statements exactly as what we term the law of gravitation is a designation and not an explanation.

The ordinary theory is that known as psycho-physical parallelism, or the double aspect. According to this theory, physical changes accompany, and are simultaneous with, psychical facts. The psychical facts are one side of the shield, the physical facts the other, and yet the physical facts can be explained by physical causes, the mental by psychical causes.

Now whatever other merits this theory may have, it has, in some of its forms at least, the demerit of absolute unintelligibility. We can understand two sets of physical causes combining to produce a result; but we are here asked to hold (1) that two sets of facts, separated by an impermeable bulkhead, and absolutely heterogeneous in their natures, are determined each by their individual chains of causation, but that (2) the changes in the one chain correspond to the changes in the other chain in the sense that a given psychical change is always accompanied by a corresponding physical change, and that the changes and results may be described indifferently in terms of mind or matter.

As long as psychology puts mind and matter in separate compartments and keeps them there, it is clearly rather unreasonable to ask psychical research to propound a physical theory of certain changes in mental states. If mind is a thing *sui generis* with its own chain of causation, it is surely enough to say that mind influences mind, for *ex hypothesi* matter does not matter. We know certain of the steps by which mind is seen to influence mind in ordinary life. The modes by which this influence is exerted we call written and spoken language, gesture and so on, but as to the process, so far as the passage from the mental to the physical and from the physical back to the mental is concerned, we are completely in the dark.

All we can give an account of, are certain physical processes, beginning, to take the typical cases speaking and writing with their correlatives, hearing and reading, as a matter of experience with nervous changes, as a matter of theory with antecedent brain changes, none of which have, however, ever been observed, and possibly never will be observed; proceeding as muscular changes, by means of which at some time, proximate or remote, gaseous matter is set in a state of vibration or solid matter receives more or less permanent impressions; continued as nervous vibrations and, again in theory and not as a matter of observation, terminating, so far as the physical world is concerned, in brain changes. The important point, the link between mental and brain changes at the outset and brain and mental changes at the close, is left absolutely untouched.

But this means that psychology and physiology have not explained how mind influences mind indirectly. All they have done is to leave the mental element out of account and trace certain chains of physical causation. But if science can give no explanation of the transmission of thought in the field which she investigates, it is clearly unreasonable to demand that, as a preliminary to the investigation of evidence going to show the existence of other modes of mental interaction, possibly entirely non-physical, a theory shall be set forth which assumes that a chain of physical causation *does* form a part of the process.

If we glance for a moment at the facts on which we base our belief that one man can communicate with another, we find that, under certain circumstances, we are able, by means of a process, the intermediate portion of which is physical, the beginning and end psychical, in its nature, to transmit our thoughts, according to universal belief, from one to another by speech or writing. We conclude that we are able to do so, not because we are able to trace part of the process in the physical world and there observe certain invariable sequences, and to assume similar sequences in portions of the physical world withdrawn from observation, but because we find that, under favourable circumstances, the thought which we express evokes a response from a being whose consciousness we infer, resembles our own, a response in harmony with the expectations we have formed. The fact that we cannot make a deaf man or a foreigner understand us at all and that we not infrequently make other apparently normal individuals, speaking our own tongue, understand us only with considerable difficulty, does not affect our judgment on the question, which does not depend on any fact, except that the number of coincidences which we infer to exist between the mental images of other people and our own is greater than it would be if the two series of phenomena were as absolutely independent of one another as any two series can be in the same universe.   If we fail to make a fellow countryman understand, we conclude, either that he is dull-witted or that his attention is distracted, or, at any rate, not devoted either wholly or to a sufficient extent to the matter of our communication, whether this be due to external causes such as distance or noise, to physiological causes, such as bodily impediments to the normal operation of the ordinary chains of causation which result in sight or hearing, or to mental causes such as absorption in some other idea; or, if we do not look for the cause of the failure to transmit our ideas either in the physical conditions or in the individual whom we are addressing, we conclude that our language has been ill-chosen, or that the ideas are in themselves difficult to understand if not entirely incomprehensible.

It is, therefore, not on any supposed explanation of the mechanism of the communication of ideas that we base our belief in its possibility.   This explanation science cannot give in its entirety.

In dealing with the ordinary processes by which we transmit our thoughts, science is able to trace only a part of the process; but an incomplete chain of causation does not explain a process, any more than a broken chain will transmit a pull; science cannot claim to have made transmission of thought by language more intelligible or more easy to accept as a fact by showing that certain links can be explained. In the second place, our judgment in the matter does not depend on the completeness or otherwise with which we can explain the process from its beginning in the mind through certain physical changes to its end in another mind. So far as the proof of the transmission is concerned, we may disregard the ability of the physicist and the physiologist to show us that waves of light or sound and sensory and motor impulses stand to one another in the relation of cause and effect. We conclude that we can transmit our thoughts, because, on a rough estimate, we succeed immeasurably oftener than we fail, and our successes are far more numerous than can be accounted for by chance and the laws of normal variation.

Now, it is clear that we cannot demand more evidence for thought transference than we do for ordinary transmission of thought. If the one process cannot be completely explained, no one has a right to accept it as a fact, and at the same time to refuse to credit the existence of another process, because this second process, unlike the first, does not receive even a partial explanation in terms of physics and physiology. Even if the second process were known to be partially physical, the absence of an explanation would be no logical bar to its acceptance as a fact. Until it is shown to be partially physical, the absence of such explanation is an even less valid argument for not admitting the existence of the fact. A fact is not less a fact because it is unexplained. The proof of thought transference, resting on an unexplained excess of coincidences in the mental phenomena of two individuals, is valid so far as the investigations are successful in excluding all transmission by means of the senses, whether they offer or succeed in giving an explanation of the process of thought transference or not. Not only is it perfectly legitimate first to prove the fact and then to seek the explanation, but we may, as we do and have done for years in the case of gravitation, accept this fact and investigate its laws, without holding, or attempting to formulate any theory, physical or otherwise, as to its mode of operation.

CHAPTER XII

How to experiment

IN the hope that some leisured reader, who is also endowed with inexhaustible patience, may be induced by a perusal of the foregoing pages to try some experiments on his own account, I now offer some suggestions as to the methods of experimentation. The errors have been alluded to already, for the most part, in the running discussion on the series of trials described above. It will, however, be convenient to collect the scattered hints and give precise directions for avoiding causes of error.

First, as to the object, that is to say, the word, idea, diagram, picture, or whatever may be selected for the agent to transfer mentally to the percipient. Except in the case of pictures, complicated objects should be avoided, as being unnecessarily hard for the agent to grasp and unlikely to be reproduced by any except unusually gifted percipients.

Where the object is a card or something equally readily drawn at random from a number of apparently similar objects, no special precautions need be taken except to thoroughly shuffle the pack after each draw; this will be most easily done if two packs are used. Where the object cannot be selected in this way, care should be taken to eliminate any personal element by making the choice depend on the toss of a coin, or by numbering the objects and deciding on the number by drawing lots. This can be readily done by having two boxes of cards with numbered digits, the second containing all ten figures, the first only so many as are required to make it possible to draw any of the objects but no more. Cloak room tickets can of course be used; it will save trouble to sort out only the precise number wanted.

Where diagrams are used care should be taken to prepare them beforehand so that they can be selected by lot or drawn like ordinary playing cards. Calculations of probabilities are simplified by the use of round numbers, fifty or a hundred. If the number in use is too large, there is apt to be a great similiarity between two or more diagrams, which upsets the calculation of probabilities.

Next as to the locale of the experiments. Two rooms should be used, for, especially with unskilled experimenters, it is by no means easy to avoid verbal suggestion. The signal for the commencement of the experiment should be given by a bell or some means that does not involve personal communication; it is not difficult to rig up two electric bells, so that both agent and percipient can signal. If only one bell is used, a given time must be agreed on for each experiment. It saves trouble to try the experiments in series of ten, or, in the case of cards, thirteen or twenty-six.

Then as to methods. Crystal gazers or automatic writers may use these methods of externalizing their impressions. For the ordinary person only two forms of experiment or at most three are available. They may wait for a mental impression, that is to say, make their minds as much a blank as possible and guess whatever comes into their heads after the signal has been given. Or, if they are expert visualisers, that is to say, if they can without difficulty call up a vivid mental picture of an object, such as we nearly all of us see in dreams, by merely thinking of it, they can close their eyes and endeavour to keep their mental blackboard a blank until the signal has been given, and then either describe what they see to a third person, or, especially if they are handy with the pencil, sketch what they see on a numbered piece of paper.

Some few people seem to get auditory impressions, that is to say, it is as though the word or idea were whispered to them. No special precautions are needed in such cases.

If it is important to take all these measures, in order to prevent causes of error, it is no less important to record that they have been taken, otherwise the experiments are valueless as a contribution to science. However persuaded the experimenter may be in his own mind that there were no disturbing elements, his assurance on this point carries no weight unless he can point to the corroborative testimony of the contemporaneous record. Especially where the experimenters have no great experience in such matters, it is well to depute one person to keep the record and to do nothing else. This is, of course, a simple matter where agent and percipient are in different rooms (in which case two recorders are needed), but even then it is far less simple than it seems to take accurate notes of all that goes on, and especially of any communication between the two rooms.

The record should be absolutely contemporaneous; any subsequent additions must be clearly distinguished as such. It must give details of time and place, of the names of all present, of the objects used in the experiments, and of how the selection of each object for the individual experiments was made. It should state whether the percipient was aware what kind of trial—whether with cards, numbers or what not—was being made, whether he was previously acquainted with the diagrams or informed of the limits between which the numbers lay, and so on. It should be noted whether the percipient concentrated his attention on the object, or closed his eyes and tried to visualise it, and so on. The percipient's words should be taken down verbatim, together with details as to the method of externalization, crystal automatic writing, etc. In fact it is very easy to note too little, but difficult to note too much.

The records should be dated and signed by the recorder, and carefully preserved for analysis, whether the series is in any way successful or not, as data for the study of thought transference. Any one who gets, or believes that he gets, results considerably above expectation for any period of time, will do well to communicate with the Society for Psychical Research, which will control the results by further sittings, if desirable.

It is a convenient plan, especially in card experiments, to enter on the same sheet the cards drawn and the guesses.

As an illustration of the way in which the record is kept, I append a copy of one of a duplex experiment. The experimenters were all familiar with the routine of experiments, and consequently the only facts to be recorded were the positions of the experimenters, the object, the guesses, and the way in which the record was kept.

20, Hanover Square, W., 4.40 p.m., February 2, 1903. Conditions as before.

P

Percipients, Mrs. H., in the library; Mr. Thomas, in store-room.

Agent, Miss R., in secretary's room.

V. Larminie recording. Two packs used; card drawn, ring and record. Series of thirteen before comparing—

Card Drawn.	Mrs. H.	Mr. T.
1. 7 H.	6 D.	2 D.
2. 9 D.	Kn. H.	6 H.
3. Kn. Sp.	6 C.	5 S ¼
4. Kn. Sp.	9 Sp. ¼	4 C.
5. 8 C.	7 H.	9 D.
6. 4 C.	1 C. ¼	Kg S.
7. Kn. D.	7 H. cor. to 6D ⅛	4 H.
8. 6 S.	4 H.	Qn. C.
9. 10 H.	Kg. S.	10 H. $\frac{1}{52}$
10. 9 S.	5 C.	7 C.
11. 2 H.	10 H ¼	6 S.
12. 6 S.	Kg. S. ¼	1 S. ¼
13. 4 C.	4 C. $\frac{1}{52}$	4 C. $\frac{1}{52}$

In this table the first column is that kept by the recorder during the progress of the experiments; the second and third are entered subsequently from the cards kept by the percipients or the recorders who kept notes of what they say. The figures show the consequences, $\frac{1}{52}$ = card right, $\frac{1}{13}$ = number right, ¼ = suit right, these fractions representing expectation.

BIBLIOGRAPHY

Proceedings of the S.P.R.
      Vol. i. pp. 13, 35, 43, 47, 70, 161,* 263.*
           ii. pp. 1, 24,* 189, 239.*
           iii. pp. 190, 424.*
           iv. pp. 127,* 324.
           v. pp. 18,* 169, 216,* 269, 355.
           vi. pp. 128,* 398.
           vii. pp. 3, 374.
           viii. pp. 422, 536.*
           x. 14.*
           xi. pp. 2, 235.
           xii. 298.*

Journal of the S.P.R.
      Vol. i. pp. 318, 419, 460.
           ii. 34, 93, 183.
           iii. 179, 182, 186,* 190, 259, 309.
           iv. 33, 303.
           v. 21, 51, 111, 167, 182, 184, 189, 266, 276, 293.
           vi. 4, 7, 98, 175, 227, 296.
           vii. pp. 5, 34, 179, 234, 325.*
           viii. p. 302.

Proceedings American S.P.R. Vol. i,

  Ochorowicz. *La Suggestion Mentale*, Paris, 1887.

  *Podmore, F. *Apparitions and Thought Transference*, London, 1894.

  Podmore, Gurney and Myers, *Phantasms of the Living*, London, 1885.

. *Revue Philosophique*, xviii. 609; xxiii. 400; xxii. 208; xxv. 435.

Blackburn, D., *Thought Reading*, London, 1884.

In addition to the above list, which does not profess to be in any way exhaustive, there are many articles, chiefly of an ephemeral nature, in contemporary literature, reference to which will be found in Poole's *Catalogue*.

In the above list the important articles are marked with an asterisk.

INDEX